Dear Kennedy

Dear Kennedy

▲ Dedication

▲ Introduction

▲ Chapter 1 - Dear Mom, I Wish I Could Have Understood

▲ Chapter 2 - Her

▲ Chapter 3 - Sweet Sixteen

▲ Chapter 4 - A Woman and Her Work

▲ Chapter 5 - A Woman and Her God

▲ Chapter 6 - A Woman and Her Ministry

▲ Chapter 7 - A Woman and Her Relationships

▲ Chapter 8 - A Woman and Her Marriage

▲ Chapter 9 - A Woman and Her Children

▲ Chapter 10 - A Woman and Herself

▲ Chapter 11 - Miss Misunderstood

▲ Chapter 12 - The "In-Between" Experiences

▲ Chapter13 - The Story of Seasons

▲ Chapter 14 - Be Authentic

▲ Chapter 15 - Ask for The Lord's Guidance

▲ Chapter 16 - Establish Your Values

▲ Chapter 17 - Do Not Be Afraid

▲ Chapter 18 - Joy in The Journey

▲ Chapter 19 - Life Is About Dancing in The Rain

▲ Chapter 20 - Delay Gratification and Live Generously

▲ Chapter 21 -Forever Friends

▲ Chapter 22- Forgiving the Bottle

▲ Chapter 23 - The Truths About Love

▲ Chapter 24 - Identity and The Anorexic

▲ Chapter 25 - The Security of Pain

▲ Chapter 26 - Brotherly Love

▲ Chapter 27 - Holding On

▲ Contributing authors:

Kristin Flynn

Kristen Cottingham

Rachel Zito

Sarah Webb

Amanda Sorrelle

Kim Qualls

Jenny Walther

Nancy Staffeld

Lindsey Seelye

Rachel Phelps

"A lot of people just need someone to be kind to them today."

Dedication

For my father.

You are my best friend, my rock, my healer, and my provider. Thank you for taking on the toughest role in our household, playing both the mother and father part. It isn't easy, life throws curveball after curveball. But every single day you show me the power of perseverance and love in a life of following Jesus.

Introduction

Even if you don't want to admit it right now, we all have an expiration date. Coming to terms with the fact that we all die someday can be daunting, and it might even sound a little bleak. Time slowly ticks away, and before we even have time to realize, life as we know it is over. The more we make of the life we have, the scarier it is to think about losing it. To some people, the thought of death is alarming and frightening but to others, approaching death comes with a sense of peace due to their faith and hope of what could be on the other side.

We are all just chasing daylight. As soon as we are fully aware of the life we live and the blessings we receive every day, we become fully aware of death and how we can lose people and even ourselves at any moment. I am not trying to start this book out on a dispiriting note; in fact, the awareness of death can work in our favor. When we understand that at any moment, we could lose the people we love, we develop a different sense of appreciation and love for those dear to us.

The event of death itself is devastating, but sometimes we seem to forget all the baggage that comes with it. Baggage that includes grief, family drama, depression, dealing with the loss loved one's belongings and so much more. Usually, when someone dies, it causes a sort of domino effect. Things change drastically before we even realize it.

It was really quite strange how it all happened. The death of my mother, that is—the moments leading up to it, what my mother felt and went through, how people around us were affected, and the way we coped with and rationalize the situation. My mother's journey toward her own death started when she was young, with sexual and emotional trauma becoming precipitating factors pushing her to a life of destructive coping habits. This unfortunate experience led her to seek refuge from that experience by falling into an eating disorder and alcoholism as an attempt at seeking shelter from the pain. Neither provided the emotional relief my mother sought.

Nonetheless, from the ashes of that early childhood came a beautiful story of being saved by God's grace, even though this story is of a very broken, anorexic, alcoholic. Somehow this story became mine to tell after she passed.

Genetics can be funny in that way. God is funny in that way. I wish it could be my mom writing this book and sharing her story of overcoming anorexia, depression, alcoholism, and sleep deprivation. But she is now in heaven, encouraging me to write this story and how it all came to be.

She used to always tell me that someday she would "write a book" and that she had so many "stories and adventures that needed to be heard. Everyone does. We are most human when we are connected with each other and spreading love."

My mother's thought that "everyone does" resonates with me because people sharing their life stories with me put me where I am today. I'm eighteen years old writing a book about how real our Lord and Savior is. This book is about how I realized the power of kindness and compassion, and how each person can live wholly and directly on God's grace. This book isn't just about me, the women and people who stepped into my life to help, or even my mom's death. It isn't focusing on eating disorders or alcoholism. This book is about all of us as human beings and our ability to have Jesus in our hearts so He, in turn, can change lives. This book is about being human, flawed, saved, and loved. This book is about how we all fall short of the glory of God no matter who we are. I have discovered through my journey that we all have an inseparable need for love and acceptance, and we can all find it in the overwhelming love, grace, and forgiveness of Jesus Christ. I believe that all of us have the ability to love and to live a life of joy while encouraging others to do the same, just like Jesus did. That's how my mother lived her life every single day.

I know for certain that we are not called to judge, save, change, or ridicule people; we are called to love them. This book also tells the story of how some amazing women took a chance to be completely vulnerable with me and how it opened my eyes to a whole new way of life. Their prompting, along with numerous other helping hands, set me on a journey to find myself, to grow, to love, to live and breathe again. I hope this book opens your mind, challenges you, and guides you. We all have stories that need to be heard and legacies to leave behind. You hold the key to your life. Decide the life you want and create it.

I can't prove God to you. I can only guide you and tell you my story of how I got to this place, of a relationship with Jesus Christ. I can prove to you that love matters, forgiveness is important, your sense of identity is powerful, and we *belong* in community.

Chapter One

Dear Mom, I wish I could have understood

Dear Mom,

I looked up at the stands from the basketball court, and there you were. You were beaming with pride, and you gave me that look only a mother and child could understand. I could see it in your eyes that you were so proud of your little girl. And just like that, I would never see you in the stands at one of my games again.

You battled hard, but when you fell, the sound was deafening. I wish I could have understood what you were going through. I wish I had known and been wise enough to have more empathy. Looking back, things make sense now. I can remember seeing the exhaustion in your eyes and smelling alcohol on your breath. I remember the dinners you would make but never eat. The nights you would tuck us into bed, exhausted, but never sleep. The combination of your anorexia and your alcohol dependency was taking control of your life. When you had good days, you were absolutely unstoppable—super mom. But during the bad days, I felt like I almost had to be the mom.

My dear mother, I loved every part of you, flaws and all. If I had a second chance, I would make sure I told you that every single day. I would encourage you to take off your mask of "perfect mom" and listen. I would urge you to get help and tell you honestly how I felt. Mom, I would thank you for the foundation of Christ, strength, and love you laid out for me at such a young age. I would thank you for the countless car rides, meals, laughs, and cries. I would hug you tighter, snuggle with you longer, and tell you I love you a lot more.

Mom, I am so sorry. I am so sorry you were hurting, and we didn't know how to help. I am so sorry for the grudges I held and the words I said. But, mom, I want you to know that this book is for you. Your legacy will live on every single day. The lives you have touched and continue to touch because of how you and dad taught Karson, Parker (my brothers), and I the art of compassion. Your selfless life consumed of serving others is living on.

I cannot thank you enough for showing me that being a follower of Jesus was more than going to church, trying not to cuss, and singing a couple of worship songs. You showed me from such a young age that the God of the universe, the creator of the stars and galaxies, loves us with a radical, unconditional, self-sacrificing love. Thank you for loving me every day of your life, the way God loves us.

Until we meet again,
Kennedy

Chapter Two
Her

"Kennedy just trust me. Everything is going to be completely fine!"

I looked at my mom and shrugged, *"Whatever."*

She pulled over to the curb in front of Target and began speaking to an older woman who ran right out in front of the car begging for help. She needed a ride to her family members house and had no money for the bus or a cab.

I knew as soon as my mom got out of the car, this woman would be in the front seat in a matter of minutes. Of course, we were going to give her a ride, why wouldn't we trust just any stranger on the street? I watched my mom nod at me, signaling for me to move to the back seat with my little brother. Then the woman climbed in.

"Thank you so much! I am so sorry to bother you folks. Oooh! Those are some beautiful kiddos you got!"

My brother and I smiled. She was kind and seemed extremely thankful. As the car ride continued, my mom became immersed in a deep conversation with this woman about music and the power of worship. Come to find out, the woman was a gospel singer originally from the South but was here visiting with family in Kalamazoo. While she was out, she got a little turned around and couldn't figure out her way back home. Thank the good Lord for GPS! Soon the car was filled with her soulful music as she belted out lyrics from her favorite songs and even some of her originals. She had a beautiful voice and used it to entertain us during the ride. As we arrived at her destination, I remember her telling us that she would be sending us a copy of her new CD when it was released. We said "Goodbye" and "Good luck" and "God bless." As our new friend departed, my mom adjusted the rearview mirror and smirked.

"Another story for my book, Kennedy!"

I rolled my eyes a little bit because of course, it would be in her book, along with the millions of other crazy things that had happened in her life. She was one of a kind, she loved deeply and consistently, but this was just another day for her. As my mom drove off, I remember wondering, how will she even find our address to send us the CD?

Fast forward ten years. We never got the CD. Bummed? Yes, me too.

But that's not what this whole little story is about. This story is about my mother. This little adventure and spur-of-the-moment service was pretty much her ministry. Any time she felt called to move, she moved. I wish I could count how many times we gave a ride to a homeless person, dropped off food or mittens to people on the side of the streets, or suddenly heard someone's life story in the middle of a convenience store. It was as if my mom had this magnet that attracted people in need. People gravitated toward her, and she gravitated toward people. Each person she met was greeted with her beautiful smile and the feeling of immediate connection. She was special.

It didn't matter that we never got the CD. What mattered was my mom helping someone who was in need, without question, without a second thought, she just served. My mother lived a life that wasn't about the physical things she acquired or money she made; it was about the people she helped. It was about who she lifted up that day, who she could be a light for, who she could love and encourage. She knew that everyone in life needs help sometimes, because she needed it too. But as you will find out later, she was too afraid to ask for it. Before she began to fall, she lived a life like Jesus, unafraid of the judgments of other people and wholeheartedly aware of what the Holy Spirit was telling her. She served people who were the most different from her. She loved the people who hurt her the most and forgave those who seemed to be so unforgivable. But when things got messy, they really got messy.

Her mental illness bound her to the idea that she could walk through life without the help of her husband, parents, friends, family, or children. She hung on to the thought that she needed to fix and help other people before herself. But when we choose to cope and look at ourselves through the wrong lens and cling to substances or unhealthy mental thoughts, our lives can become completely destructive and sad.

My mom battled the tough internal demons of alcohol dependency, anorexia, and depression. Mental health is what fuels our physical health and our life. Spiritual and emotional health is the fuel that allows your light to shine. I hope this book will open your eyes to how we should be nourishing every aspect of our life with the help of Jesus, human connection, and love so in turn we can create a life full of unexplainable peace and joy.

Chapter Three
Sweet Sixteen

Tim Elmore, president and founder of Growing Leaders, international speaker, and best-selling author described a rite of passage he and his wife provided for their teenage daughter, Bethany, as she ventured into high school. He shares that a rite of passage is an experience or ceremony that has existed in many cultures throughout history. The rite of passage Tim Elmore and his wife designed for their daughter required choosing a handful of women with a variety of backgrounds and experiences to be "one-day mentors" for their daughter that year. They asked the woman who was the mentor of the day to share one life lesson with their daughter—a lesson they wish someone had shared with them but never did.

Unbeknownst to me, some women who were moms, professionals, community leaders, and women of deep faith were being recruited for a version of this rite of passage following my mother's death. Many of these women I knew only at a surface level, but I would come to know them in such a deep and loving way while celebrating my sixteenth birthday.

The rite of passage event was a surprise birthday dinner and included seven women. Their sole purpose that evening, other than celebrating my sixteenth birthday, was to formally invite me into the ranks of womanhood, to help me transition as an emerging adult by moving beyond childhood and accepting responsibility for my own spiritual growth.

Before the birthday dinner event, each woman was asked to write a short letter to me on the assigned topic and then to read it during the evening celebration and present some small gift that was symbolic of her charge. These were the assigned topics:

- A Woman and Her Work
- A Woman and Her God
- A Woman and Her Ministry
- A Woman and Her Relationships
- A Woman and Her Marriage
- A Woman and Her Children
- A Woman and Herself

The women hoped that by sharing their experiences and offering their ongoing support, they would help me in my desires for womanhood and acceptance of responsibility for future spiritual growth. Before each woman read her assigned letter, they all prayed blessings over me. Several of the women in attendance did not know one another until that evening. God delivered with His protection, grace, and blessings during the evening in a way that I would not fully understand until years later.

The tradition continued for my eighteenth birthday with the women as they remembered when they went off to college and shared their failures and life advice. The letters they wrote, the words said, the tears shed, and the hugs given have caused a radical change in my life. But before I could fully embrace who I was, I had to fall down a few times, just as each of them had done before me. There was a meaningful connection formed between us all because these women bravely shared their truth, and for that, I am forever thankful. Vulnerability is the heart of connection, and connection is the heart of our world.

This book comes from trusting Him in my dark places. Trusting Him to use my story to build His kingdom. But if these women had never reached out to me, I am not sure I would even be here writing to you. So here they are, the glorious letters that changed my life forever. I encourage you to apply these letters to your life and find ways to relate them to your current circumstances, no matter where you may be on your faith journey or who you are. Allow the Lord to open your heart to see different perspectives, words of encouragement, and advice.

Chapter Four

A Woman and Her Work

Dear Kennedy,

In your young life, you have already overcome challenges that most young women never have to endure. Your story is rich with experiences, some more painful than words can describe. These experiences have taught you something very important about yourself—what it's like to feel pain, sadness, fear, and grief. This understanding you have can be shared by very few sixteen-year-old women. As difficult as it has been and will continue to be for you, this awareness allows you to have depth, a depth of understanding regarding what's meaningful about life, the depth of feeling another person's pain, the depth to really see people who struggle and understand how that might feel. You have compassion, strength, endurance, struggle, and authenticity. You didn't ask for it, but God allowed you the opportunity to learn the depths of these things in your soul.

I am a counselor, and one of my favorite Scripture passages, and one that inspires my work, is 2 Corinthians 1:3 (NIV).

> *Praise to the God of All Comfort. "Praise be to the God and Father of our Lord Jesus Christ, the Father of compassion and the God of all comfort, who comforts us in all our troubles, so that we can comfort those in any trouble with the comfort*

we ourselves receive from God. For just as we share abundantly in the sufferings of Christ, so also our comfort abounds through Christ.

I want to encourage you to pursue a career that is a natural reflection of your identity. Pursue work that allows your story, your experience to sing. Find work that allows you to be compassionate, to show strength, perseverance, and love. Know that God has started a good work in you. He has a purpose for your life. He created you in perfection and, despite the pain life brings, will constantly work to return you to perfection. As the apostle Paul wrote in Philippians 1:4, 6 *"I always pray with joy...being confident in this, that he who began a good work in you will carry it on to completion until the day of Christ Jesus"* This task I have charged you with begins with learning and discovering who you are (this took me a little time in my own life). Discover yourself through being part of a team, being a good friend, volunteering, and working. Notice your passion. Notice what inspires you. Notice what hurts you and notice what makes you feel strong. This is discovering who you are. Now go and be her, the beautiful, strong, inspiring woman God has already created you to be.

Your friend,

Sarah

Chapter Five

A Woman and Her God

Dear Kennedy,

Every aspect of your life is affected by your relationship with God. The world offers temporary solutions, temporary relief, temporary satisfaction. Only God can give you "abundant life"; He never fails, He never leaves, and He is your Rock and everlasting Joy. Make your Savior the center of your life. Through the good parts, give Him praise. Through the rough parts, give Him praise. God has everything to offer to those who continue to seek Him. PRAY! Prayer is your lifeline. God wants more than anything to hear from you. He can take it...all your hopes, disappointments, and questions. He wants to hear it all from you! Read His Word! You won't find answers without looking in His Word. Let Him lead! Seek His will for your life. He will lead...you need to follow! There won't always be a big neon sign pointing you in a certain direction, but He will clear a path for you to follow. Trust! Trust in God—He won't let you down.

I am at rest in God alone; my salvation comes from him. He alone is my rock and my salvation, my stronghold; I will never be shaken. —Psalm 62:1-2, CSB

Love the Lord your God with all your heart, with all your soul, and with all your mind, and all your strength. —Mark 12:30, CSB

You will call to me and come and pray to me, and I will listen to you. You will seek me and find me when you search for me with all your heart. —Jeremiah 29:12-13, CSB

Love,

Rachel

Chapter Six

A Woman and Her Ministry

Dear Kennedy,

I often see you in the halls at church, and there are many things I want to say but just don't know how. So, I give you a hug and a smile, and we go on our way. I am SO happy to have the opportunity to be a part of this evening and to share my thoughts with you about life in ministry! I started my ministry journey at Connections Community Church by volunteering to serve with the kids. What started as helping led to teaching, and that eventually led to leading. When you say YES to God, it always starts a chain reaction like that!

I remember I would arrive at church early to set up, and you were always there early, too, with your mom. You must have been about six or seven at the time; gosh, you were such a little sweetie! My husband and I always used to say, "That little Kennedy...she's so cute!" I remember you being willing to help with whatever I asked, and you did it with a smile on your face every time. I will forever remember you as one of my "go-to" kids, the ones you can count on to participate, include others, and have a true servant's heart!

As my role in ministry evolved over the years, so did my idea of what it meant to serve in ministry. There are three big ideas that

I've come to understand over the years of working at Connections!

The First Big Idea: Your Ministry Is Not Just at Church!

I think when most people hear the word ministry, they automatically apply it to church or mission work. We are called to minister in every area of our lives. Let your family, school, friends, workplace, team, and so on all be areas in which you honor God by sharing the love of Christ. You will have to call on God for discernment in these areas. People will receive what you have to tell them in different ways. Remember what *1 Timothy 4:12* tells us. *Don't let anyone think less of you because you are young. Be an example to all believers in what you say, in the way you live, in your love, in your faith, and in your purity (NIV).*

The Second Big Idea: Your Ministry Is All About People!

This is one of my favorite lessons learned over the years, and your mom had a huge part in helping me see it. I used to put so many hours into planning Sunday morning lessons, finding props, making sets, preparing crafts, learning new games...the list goes on. What I was trying to do was make the ministry better by making the experiences better. It was hard to do in a rented building, and I felt limited by that fact. What I failed to see was that while all these things are good, my approach was wrong. Ministry is never about programming or a building. I am reminded of *2 Corinthians 5:18: "God has given us this task of reconciling people to him" (NLT)*. It's all about reaching people and helping them connect to Christ and His purpose for their lives. Relationships always come first! It is by nurturing relationships with people you serve and the volunteers you serve alongside that a ministry can become fully effective. Your mom was great at this, and I learned a lot from her.

The Third Big Idea: You Were Designed for a Specific Role in Ministry!

I love how The Message communicates

1 Corinthians 12:27:

"You are Christ's body—that's who you are! You must never forget this. Only as you accept your part of that body does your 'part' mean anything."

This is an area that I am extremely passionate about and would love to discuss more at another time if you're ever interested. You were designed on purpose with a unique set of strengths. Those strengths are influenced and made more unique by your individual personality. I encourage you to spend some time contemplating this and revisit it from time to time. You must be able to take a real honest look at things you are good at and nurture those things to become who God created you to be. I spent years being focused on the things that I wasn't good at, and that often left me feeling like I didn't measure up. I had a pretty major perspective shift several years ago when I was taught that it was more important to nurture my strengths than to try and improve my weaknesses.

Part of figuring out who God designed you to be is taking action! Test yourself by getting involved in your church and your community. Growth only comes when you give it a chance. So, try things. Don't be afraid to screw up...you will. Don't ever believe you have to have it all figured out. Just commit yourself to a life of learning from your failure as much as your success.

Lots of love always,

Lindsey

Chapter Seven

A Woman and Her Relationships

Dear Kennedy,

One of the most profound pieces of advice about relationships I ever received was about building a wisdom team. Simply put, who are the right teammates to build you up when you're down, pick you up when you stumble, guide you when you're uncertain, and confront you when you're out of bounds? Who will pour God's wisdom into your mind and heart and be with you during the thick and thin times? While the people who are part of your wisdom team may come and go over the years, I have learned that a dream team has four key relationships: Walker, Warrior, Watchman, and Workman. It's this mix of people you need to surround yourself with while doing life.

The Walker is you. This is really defined by your personal relationship with Jesus. You are the only one who can make the choice of whether that relationship is moving closer or further away. Some days, or even seasons of your life, the relationship may be more difficult to sustain. This is when you must reset your life and put proper accountability checks in place to move closer to Jesus, as He is the only One who is timeless and will sustain you through any storm. As you walk through your life, walk with Him. The closer you are, the consistency will be the key relationship you can count on when others in your life may have an ebb and flow to them.

The Warrior is a peer. This is a friend or two that is willing to stand with you, side by side, throughout life. We need someone who will love us unconditionally and hold our feet to the fire to help us pursue our purpose. This is the person (or people) who say, "I believe in you!" The Warrior keeps believing in you until you believe in yourself—in your God-given gifts and abilities that will lead you toward the purpose of your life. What happens over time with a Warrior or two in your life is that you become a Warrior too, building up and believing in others. It's a beautiful, magical flow of growing and empowering others by helping them step out of their comfort zone to a growth zone and toward that beautiful purpose in a person's life.

The Watchman is a mentor. This is a woman who is a season or two removed from you, kind of like the women we have gathered here tonight...your tribe. I have been fortunate enough to have some amazing Watchmen in my life. I intentionally seek relationships with women ten to twenty years younger and older. The older, wiser ones can invest in us by sharing their mistakes and life advice and by helping us create our own personal networks of relationships. The younger ones become their Workmen.

The Workman is a disciple. At its essence, it's you pouring into other people, specifically women, what God and your mom have poured into you. As women, we often sell ourselves short. We have so much to offer others. We don't need to be perfect to invest in others; we just need a willing heart. Please remember this point over time. None of us are perfect, and we all make mistakes, but that doesn't prevent us from reaching out, meeting a need, praying with someone, offering a helping hand or a kind word, or letting someone know how grateful we are for a contribution she has made to our lives.

Tonight's event would not have come together without this imperfect person and a heart willing to reach out to you and somehow ease the pain of losing your mom as we celebrate this milestone birthday. When you have a Workman, you become that person's Watchman.

Proverbs 18:1 warns us not to isolate ourselves, which results in our making foolish decisions and wasting time. Isolation is the silent enemy and always ends in regret. To live the life, you were meant to live, these four key relationships are essential.

While you have this team of women as part of your life, be intentional with any others you assemble. Ask God to reveal who should be a part of your wisdom team and continually have a network of these relationships throughout your life, even if that means that players on your team change from time to time as you enter a new season or phase of life.

Aside from a deep relationship with Jesus, having a loving relationship with yourself is another important relationship. So, look at all your good qualities and decide to love yourself exactly the way you are right now. Learning to do this through all of life is a battle. The greatest battles you will ever fight in your life are between your ears. It's true that your mind is often your biggest battlefield. If you can win that battle over time, not listening to your inner critic, your relationship with others and with yourself allows you to live a full life, a purposeful life, a life God intended you to live.

I am so thankful that I have gotten to know you and look forward to our ongoing relationship, knowing that God is planning something really big for your life. Happy sixteenth birthday!

Love you,

Kristin

Chapter Eight

A Woman and Her Marriage

Dear Kennedy,

First, I want you to know that you can feel free to contact me whenever or wherever and I will be there for you...seriously! Call, email, text, write (who does that anymore?!), etc. I promise I will be there on the other end. Now onto the good stuff...

When I was your age, I had a ton of questions about guys, dating, my future husband, and so on. In this letter I am giving to you today, just before your sixteenth birthday, I am including some steps to be a godly wife (that you can even start right now!). Honestly, it's not the perfect guide, but it will at least get you started, and you can fill in the gaps later.

1) ALWAYS, always, always, always keep God first! Having a man in your life (while it's nice to have a helpmate and someone to cuddle up with) is not an end-all, be-all. I remember thinking that having a husband would be so perfect! Although it is exciting and fun and can be such a blessing, husbands are human. With being human comes their sins, their issues, their baggage, and so on. Because men are human, having a man in your life is not always a bed of roses!

By keeping God at the center of your life and focus, you will not lose sight of the purpose and plans God has for your life. After all, that's why each and every one of us is here, right?

2) Guard your heart! Proverbs 4:23 says *"Above all else, guard your heart, for everything you do flows from it"* (NIV). If God is guarding your heart because you've asked Him to, you will not find yourself down a path you should not be on. Asking God to guard your heart will also save you from a lot of heartache.

3) Keep yourself pure. Society today promotes sex like crazy! The reasons range from gaining experience, so you don't look stupid on your wedding night, to "you're young and you should be able to have fun before you settle down" to "you're an uber-nerd if you're forty and still a virgin!"

But, let's be real, the truth is that every time you give yourself away, you lose a little piece of you that you can never get back. God's ways are best, and He wants to save you from a ton of issues that come along with sex. Always remember that God is merciful, loving, and forgiving God, and the great thing is, we can ask for forgiveness and move on from our guilt. There will always be consequences, but we don't have to stay in our guilt. God doesn't want that for us either!

4) Choose wisely! It is my belief there isn't one perfect soul mate out there for you to find, so in my opinion, you don't need to worry or waste your time trying to find that one "Mr. Right." God

gives us some basic guidelines to follow, and if a guy meets those, you are free to choose whether to take the plunge. I'd certainly ask for God's guidance as well because it is a very important decision. Having said that, these are two of what I believe are the most important considerations:

A) Mr. Right needs to be a believer...preferably in line with where you are on your own spiritual journey, although that alignment is not a necessity. Second Corinthians 6:14 says, *"Do not be yoked together with unbelievers. For what do righteousness and wickedness have in common?"* (NIV). I've seen many women whose hearts are torn because not only do they have a more difficult marriage, but they also have to live with the fact that they may not be spending eternity with the one person they love most in this world. I feel for them because they are in such heartache, and yet they chose to marry that man.

B) Are you better together than you are apart? God has a purpose for both of your lives. This should be the number one focus for both of you. If you can say with all sincerity and certainty that Mr. Right fits into that purpose, encourages you in it, helps you with it, and makes you a better person, I'd say, "Go for it!"

5) Never be afraid to ask for help! I've been married for more than fifteen years, and I still don't feel like I know what I'm doing most of the time. Asking for help doesn't mean that you are inadequate; it means you're smart for gaining knowledge and wisdom from people who have been there, done that. I would

also suggest being careful who you ask when you're looking for help. Since you are a child of God, I would ask someone in God's family who you know will give you godly advice, not just what you want to hear. You can start this even now in your life for all manner of things.

I realize these may not be the things you expected or wanted to be on this list. The truth is, God's ideal for all our lives may not be what we think we want, but they protect us from so much. Please know that we love you, and we all want God's best for you!

Again, we're all here...whenever you need us!

Rachel

Chapter Nine

A Woman and Her Children

Dear Kennedy,

Happy sixteenth birthday! What an honor to be a part of your birthday celebration! I am excited for you and all that the Lord has in store for your life!

I was asked to write you a letter on motherhood. I struggled to narrow down such a broad topic and make it relevant to your life as this season seems so distant into your future. I found an article written about being a mom and thought I'd share this with you.

Naked Love by Mom Life Now blog

"She woke up crying. I ran in to find her nose spilling blood everywhere. The couch cushion, the carpet, her dress. Quickly sweeping her into my arms, I ran to the bathroom where we waited for it to end. Just the two of us stripped down to princess underwear, feet dipped in the sink as we quietly waited for the bleeding to stop. I took a warm washcloth to gently clean her naked body, only the sound of the faucet in our ears. She smiled at me.

And then another sound, ringing so loudly in my ears I could not help but weep.

"I was naked, and you clothed me."

I heard it so loud. So clear. And in that moment, I realized more than ever before the utter importance of just being a mom. Because every time I mopped another spill, broke up another fight, wiped a millionth tear...each trip to the doctor, the playground, the grocery store...the cleaning and cooking and laundry and laundry and laundry...silly dances and late-night cuddles. Calming fears and comforting pains. Praise. Pride. Celebrations over putting on underwear the right way. The tasks that often seem so trivial, the moments so mundane no one else would even care to know. Each and every time, each and every moment, it is just as though I was serving Him. The Savior Himself. That's how he sees it anyway.

"I was naked, and you clothed me."

How often does this motherhood thing tend to grab our souls and make us question, yet again, if we are enough? If our life is worth enough. "Just a mom," we so often respond. Like we are somehow less deserving. But God, He sees us doing something of unmatched importance. Our babies depend on us for everything. From food in their belly to the clothes on their backs. And, although most days we may smell like grilled cheese and old milk, He sees only beauty.

Who cares if society tells you your contribution is not enough, your life a little less worthy than praise? Does society see you at 3:00 a.m. with the sick child who does not care about your successes or awards, how much money you have made, or positions you have taken? No. It's the child who cries only for Momma, whose touch alone will bring the comfort and peace she needs.

"I was naked, and you clothed me."

I held my daughter for a long time after the bleeding stopped.
Knowing that these are the moments that are shaping both our souls.
And as I held her, I knew He was right there with us. Holding us both
in ways I never could.

He's there each day, each moment. He sees. And He smiles at my
everyday world. Because He knows that with each new load of
laundry, I am serving Him. And I am serving a much bigger purpose
than I will ever truly see.

"Then the King will say...I was hungry, and you gave Me food to eat. I
was thirsty and you gave Me water to drink. I was a stranger and you
gave me a room. I was naked and you clothed Me. I was sick and you
cared for Me. I was in prison and you came to see Me.

They will say, 'Lord, when did we see You hungry and feed You? When
did we see you thirsty and give you a drink? When did we see You a
stranger and give You a room? When did we see You naked and clothe
You? And when did we see You sick or in prison and we came to You?'
Then the King will say, 'For sure, I tell you, because you did it to one of
the least of My brothers, you have done it to Me.' - Matthew 25:35-40."

I really felt that this article above hit home on how I feel about
motherhood, but it can also be applied to anyone. Not everyone
sees or understands everything that goes on in my life or your
life, but the Lord knows it all. There will be times in your life
when your work and love go unnoticed and a feeling of loneliness
sets in. He is always there for you and always ready to pick you
up.

I also thought of your mom while reading this article because of her servant attitude. She continuously gave of herself without expecting anything in return. It was her passion and mission in life. I try to remember to work with a servant's heart and just serve the Lord in all I do, whether it is cleaning, cooking, laundry, or wiping up another spill. I know that God sees it and it is really worth it.

Below are a couple of my favorite verses about children and motherhood:

"Children are a gift from the LORD; they are a reward from him" (Psalm 127:3, NLT).

"Direct your children onto the right path, and when they are older, they will not leave it." (Proverbs 22:6, NLT).

I also love this quote from Michael Jordan and think something can be taken from it. *"I've missed more than 9,000 shots in my career. I've lost almost 300 games. Twenty-six times, I've been trusted to take the game-winning shot and missed. I've failed over and over and over again in my life. And that is why I succeed."*

I challenge you to memorize as many Bible verses as you can! I frequently pull them out from memory for struggles, praises, or to teach a lesson to one of my kids. Always look to the Bible for guidance and answers. Study it. Memorize it. Keep the Lord at the center of your life. Work to become a servant in all you do. Learn to be a great listener and always seek wise counsel, and then you will be able to make decisions that are best for you.

I think that motherhood is one of the highest challenges and honors that God can give you. It is an amazing blessing from above. Most of all remember that you have this group of women who are pulling for you and ready to share your successes and willing to help, guide, and support you in tough times. I am looking forward to watching you grow and be fulfilled with all of God's plans for your life. Happy birthday!

Love and blessings to you,

Jen

Chapter Ten
A Woman and Herself

Dear Kennedy,

As the women surrounding you tonight have poured out their hearts, they have blessed you with wisdom that will prove invaluable in the days, months, and years ahead as you navigate your own life journey. I pray you will take their lessons, experiences, advice, heartaches, joys, and dreams and use them to guide you as you follow God's path for your life. Tuck their wise words away, ponder on them, and allow them to expand your perspective and give you direction. Proverbs 4:11- 12 reminds us *"I instruct you in the way of wisdom and lead you along straight paths.12 When you walk, your steps will not be hampered; when you run, you will not stumble." (NIV)*

That is the goal of all of us gathered here today. We sincerely hope and pray that your path leads you to a fulfilled life. I am honored to be surrounded by these beautiful women who have set before you goal and ideals that will lead you in that direction. My prayer is that by sharing my experiences, I, too, can offer another perspective when it comes to understanding yourself as you move into womanhood.

It is only when you truly understand who you are in relation to the God who created you that you can live a life of fulfillment and reach your own unique potential. There are many myths, misconceptions, and marred messages thrown to us as women. We're told, "You can do it all...you can have it all..." It's impossible to reach perfection in every area! There are ideals that we should strive for—such as those that the ladies have shared with you tonight—and yet there is also an element of reality that must not be dismissed either. The reality is simply this: there will be times you will fail to reach the ideal. But understanding that failure is an event, and not a person, will allow you to pick yourself back up and keep moving forward in your journey.

God created all of us with wonder and complexity and filled us with unique talents and abilities. At the same time, we are beset with many weaknesses and prone to wander after our sinful desires. We are all a mixture of good and bad; the good fuels our dreams and passions, and the bad causes us to stumble and fall. And that is exactly what life is full of—good and bad, ups and downs, successes and failures. But the one thing that remains steady through all this is God's unchanging and unfailing character and love. Read Psalm 103:8 and understand God's nature: He is merciful and gracious; He is slow to get angry and full of unfailing love.

My challenge to you is to fall into God's loving embrace of safety and acceptance when (not if!) you fail. Deuteronomy 33:27 is such a comforting reminder that *"the eternal God is your refuge, and his everlasting arms are under you"* (NLT). Through my own sin and failures—of which there are many—I have come to understand God's love as being **SAFE**. He has shown me that

S stands for SECURE: There is nothing I could ever do that's so bad that it would make God stop loving me. No matter what you've done or where you've been, you couldn't cause God to not love you! (See Romans 8:35.)

A stands for ACCEPTED: There is nothing I can do to earn God's love. No amount of accomplishments, service, following rules, or performing good deeds will be sufficient to earn his love. He accepts me not because of what I've done but because of what His Son did on the cross. (See Ephesians 1:4.)

F stands for FORGIVEN. As Romans 8:1 says, we are *free* from condemnation. As long as I am living in this human body, I will struggle with my human condition (see Romans 7). The truth is that you and I will sin every day. God knows our worst, but He is the One who loves us best! He has simply chosen not to hold our sins against us but to erase the record and grant us the freedom in our spirits to move forward in our intimacy with Him. He desires to help us reach our full potential of bringing glory to Him. His action is called "grace." First John 1:9 says, *"If we confess our sins, he is faithful and just to forgive us our sins and to cleanse us from all unrighteousness" (ESV).* There is no reason for us to hide from Him when we sin and stumble. We simply need to fall forward into His embrace and allow Him to forgive us and put us back on the path toward right living.

E stands for ENOUGH: The word alone is *enough* to cause anxiety! We as women are constantly being bombarded with the fear of not being "enough." We wonder, Am I doing enough to be accepted by those around me? Am I OK? Merriam-Webster.com defines enough is being able to "fully meet demands, needs, or expectations. "Let me remind you that you were created with such precision, skill, design, and well-thought-out care by the same God who created mountains and flung the stars into space. He looked around and thought His beautiful world needed YOU! And when God created you, He said, "It is good, and she is enough. She lacks nothing. I just want to be with her. I enjoy being with her." God desires nothing more than a relationship with you!

That is truly what all of life boils down to—a fulfilled life is found in a relationship with God. And no matter what life's journey brings, when we understand that God loves us no matter what, we can move forward with confidence and enjoy each step of the journey! Psalm 37:23-24 tells us, *"The steps of a good [woman] are ordered by the LORD...Though [she] fall, [she] shall not be utterly cast down; For the LORD upholds [her] with His hand"* (NKJV).

May God bless you and uphold you as you journey on into womanhood!

Kristen

Chapter Eleven
Miss Misunderstood

After my first birthday dinner with these women, I thought I was going to pass out. I remember thinking, *what the hell do I do now?!* My heart ached. I missed my mom. I didn't understand why these women even wanted to be a part of my life. In my mind, I felt lonely, confused, and misunderstood. I cried and cried. I think what made me the saddest was the fact that there are people in this world who lose a parent (or both), and will never receive the type of love, advice, and guidance I got. I felt guilty. I was so undeserving.

Why me? I questioned God repeatedly.

I pondered my current situation in life. My mother and these women would have been disappointed in the woman I was choosing to be. I was a sophomore in high school who based her worth entirely on what her boyfriend, peers, and social media said. I was very insecure and negative. My heart was cold, the classic "the world is against me" teenage mindset was me to a T. There was a God-sized hole in my heart that was full of temporary forms of relief. The thought of having an honest and vulnerable relationship with God was not anywhere on the radar at this time in my life. I couldn't fully face the loss of my mother, the issues surrounding her death, and most of all, I couldn't face my own self. I was embarrassed of who I had become. I lived a life of lies. I lied to my closest friends, family members and most of all myself. But I was determined to prove I was "perfectly happy" with my decisions, new boyfriend and a new set of friends. I was so broken that I couldn't bear to set my pride aside and let anyone see how hurt I was. My heart was shattered for so many reasons. The death of my mom caused a spiral out of control in my heart. The mask I put on began to fade as I was encouraged by all these women to confront my insecurities, and fears and get to know myself on a profound level. Although, the future felt uncertain, and I was scared for the next chapter of my life without my mom, I serve a loving and graceful God who has immaculate timing.

When these women came to me with the most raw and honest advice, celebrated me, and loved me, my heart grieved. I was so undeserving of their advice and counsel. These women had no idea the mistakes I made, the way I acted or viewed myself. I blamed everything bad in my life on my mom's death, her alcoholism, and mental issues. I never took responsibility for my faith and happiness. But like all of us, I had a choice to make. I could grow through my mistakes and take responsibility for my life, or I could choose to feel badly for myself and continue to go down the wrong path. We all have a choice, we are not stuck, our pain is never permanent, we can grow and change, we are supposed to.

I read the letters again a month or so later after my dinner and began to weep. I knew then that because of them, my perspective and outlook on life was changed forever. I had knowledge and advice few girls my age had. I knew that others would benefit from this idea of a rite of passage, and even the letters these women wrote to me. I needed to act on it. So, I did. It began with my prayer life. I prayed consistently over these letters. I began trying meditation practices and changing my thought process. That's when I began to see the changes. I fully put my life in God's hands. I am so grateful our Lord isn't an "I told you so" kind of God, He's more of a "Welcome home, I've missed you. I'll fix you. I'll love you." type of God.

There were always ups and downs in this process of finding myself. And I believe I always am "finding myself", I change through each season of life. There are times where I am on top of the world, and other days it's all about just putting one foot in front of the other. During this time in my life, the best change I made to myself started with simple gestures of kindness. I began treating people the way my mother did. I reminded myself that every person I encountered was facing a battle; they felt pain and caused pain to others. They were human beings who made mistakes. It's life. But I decided that the best thing I could do was to try to hear what Jesus was saying every time I met someone. I can learn from everyone, no matter the age, gender, ethnicity, or culture; we all have something to offer the world. I saw the light in others and tried to treat them as if that's all I saw.

I noticed God's voice in my life when I chose love over hate. I discovered that God is always speaking to us through our everyday lives. He speaks through other people—even though sometimes those people don't realize it. He speaks through situations, the skies, the water, the moon, the sunsets and sunrises, signs, symbols, and most of all—our hearts.

And then, a decision must be made. Do we choose to act on what He is saying?

If you ask God to lead you, don't be surprised when He leads you to make some sacrifices, to set boundaries with yourself and others, and to let go and let God work. There will always be uncomfortable times and dark places, but it's those things that make us cling closer to God. God offers an abundance of hope even when trusting Him is hard. So, that's where this book comes from, me choosing to act on what Jesus has placed on my heart.

Chapter Twelve

The "In-Between" Experiences

These seven letters from my 16th birthday have drastically changed who I am and my values of life. At this point, I thought that I was at maximum capacity when it came to advice and was all set for the next chapter of my life. Then came the grueling, confusing high school years. Luckily, for my 18th birthday, we decided to have another dinner! This time, some new women connected with all of us and I was a little bit more mature and ready to accept this advice as what it was. But, before you read the 18th birthday letters, I want you to have a glimpse into where I was at in my life.

High school was easily some of the most puzzling, painful, and wonderful years of my life. There are always awkward 'in-between' phases when you are trying to change. Maturing and growing all come at different rates for people. I was trying to figure out who I was and where I belonged, but what never changed was the love that God has for me. Through all my experiences, pain, heartache, highs, and lows, He was there.

What these women did for me, by stepping out of their comfort zone and being completely truthful, caused me to realize the importance of good friendships. Everyone has those people after leaving their presence, you feel as if a weight has been lifted off you and you can breathe again. It's so important that we surround ourselves with these types of people. I believe we also need to cultivate those qualities within ourselves that enable us to be supporters and encouragers for others through our own unique authenticity that Jesus has created within us. I now surround myself with people who encourage me to be authentic, who make me feel valued, and who truly care for my well-being.

These letters encouraged me to become closer with my family. I began to lean into my father and tell him ALL the good and bad; the girl drama, boyfriend issues, school, sports, everything. My dad taught me that we are to seek and identify our gifts and talents through experiences and adventures. Through our toughest days, we find out what we really are capable of, and how we react to our circumstances is a true testament to our character. Using these abilities ultimately allows us to connect more deeply with other people. There will be times in life where we fall short and nothing seems to go right, but that's why we have friendships, mentors, and Jesus. My dad has taught me that my moments of complete emptiness are hidden opportunities to feel the fullness of Christ.

The letters certainly changed my outlook on life, but that didn't mean that every day and season was perfect. There were still times where I couldn't comprehend how or why my mom passed away from alcohol dependency and complications with anorexia. There were and still are times where I'm angry, sad, and lost.

I read somewhere that grief is like the ocean, it comes in waves. Sometimes the water is calm, peaceful, and still, but sometimes the water is full of raging and merciless waves. When you grieve, somedays words hurt you differently, things will pierce your heart, and questions will haunt you. A peer at school once asked, "If you don't mind me asking, what happened to your mom?" It wasn't a mean question or even inappropriately timed, it was just an honest question, but in that moment, the words stung intensely. A million thoughts raced through my head: How was I, a fifteen-year-old girl, supposed to explain that she died from complications with anorexia and substance abuse? How could this possibly have happened to my mom? God, why me? Why my family?

To be quite honest, I was embarrassed of how my mom died. I hate to admit to that, but I was young and didn't understand. This embarrassment carried with me, me for several years. I remember the look in people's eyes when I would say, "She passed away from problems with anorexia and substance issues." Some looked confused, and others looked sorry for asking. I still feel the pity in their voices, and the awkward silences after the, "wow, I am so sorry."

As I got older, I realized it was so much more than just "complications" with anorexia and alcohol. It was months that turned into years of her abusing her own body with substances and negative thoughts. It was her own internal demons telling her not to eat and when she did, to puke it all up. It was outside stressors of work, family, and social standards. It hurt me so much because my mother never saw herself the way our family and friends did. My mom was a beautiful human being, her soul was kind, and her heart lived for Jesus. She was an angel on earth. Her physical beauty extended to the way she carried herself. Her personality was exquisite and captivating. She connected with everyone because of her ability to be authentic and compassionate. I believe it was because she knew how broken she was that she was able to relate with everyone around her. She never wanted anyone to feel the pain she did. She was a fixer of all problems. She put everyone before herself.

Before my mom died physically, she lost herself mentally. She would hide her pain from the ones she loved and then act out in a distraught manner. Her actions and outbursts I now recognize were her cries out for help. It was a terrifying experience for me to see my mother become so disoriented and confused. As she got sicker, and more addicted to her alcohol and stopped eating correctly, her personality changed.

We all know that how we feel determines how we act. The unhealthy mom had extreme mood swings and hallucinations, her consumption of alcohol was excessive, and her face wore an expression of pure exhaustion; she was lost. The healthy mom was glowing, graceful, happy, and fully surrendered to Jesus. But healthy or unhealthy, she never lost sight of what was most important in life: The God she served and the family she loved.

After she passed, I had to realize that it didn't matter how my mom died, because it happened. I had to realize that there are deaths every single day. People die in numerous different ways, and it doesn't matter how because, at the end of the day, it is a loss of a precious human life. Although, anytime we lose someone we love we will still have to deal with regret, anger, guilt, and grief

I think about the moments of awkwardness and disappoint when my mom would show up at social or school events intoxicated, or the moments she would hallucinate in front of her young, naive children. I sometimes wish would have just screamed at her. Maybe if I would have yelled at her and forced her to see the disappointment on her daughter's face, it would have changed things. Would it have helped if I had talked to her during her times of hallucinations and irrational behavior? What if I had just confronted her? All these situations I held onto and in turn it caused me to feel uncomfortable with who I was. I felt so misplaced. I felt angry.

The "what if" game will only leave me dissatisfied. These letters the women wrote to me motivated me to change my disappointment to compassion and understanding. I believe that all these circumstances and heartaches have put me right here today. I believe it happened for a reason. My experiences with my mother's mental health placed a fiery passion in my heart to care more deeply for my emotional, psychological, and physical well-being. Because of her, I chose to get to know myself on a profound level so I could avoid and cope with emotions and stress the correct way.

Although, my mother knew the demons she battled, and because she knew the demons, she also knew that Jesus had a far more intricately detailed, better, and more beautiful plan for her life. She preached it to me every day. I am reminded of that daily when I see her picture on the wall in my room. I am reminded by her that we all have a story and we all carry weight on our shoulders, but God is here to take that weight upon Himself. We do not have to go through this life alone, we aren't meant to!

You have the ability to feel love and to love others. You are capable. You are called. You are worthy. You are YOU for a special reason. There is no time to pretend to be this perfect person society says you must be. We need to cultivate the authenticity between us all. The realness to the pain we feel in life; whether it be loss of a loved one, addictions, depression, eating disorders, attention disorders, bullying etc. —whatever it may be! You need to know that you have been given this life with specific problems and pain for a reason. Your life is a magnificent work of art bound together by your experiences. Up until now, you have survived so many hardships and will continue to do so. You are not alone. You are loved. Your story is a beautiful, and owning your story, the hard things and easy things, is brave. Life isn't easy, but that's why we love, forgive, and have hope.

The women who picked me up after my mom's death have inspired me to be the most authentic version of myself because I never know who will need to hear my words—just as these women had no idea how much their words would help me get through life. Jesus knows you aren't perfect- Hello! That's why He died for us! We are corrupt and mad and mess up sometimes, but there is a beauty in that brokenness. Jesus died for the women and men whose hearts are aching right now and who have a restless soul. Jesus died for our sins. That means He died for our wrongdoings, evil, wickedness, transgressions, crimes, and offenses, so that we could be forgiven. Jesus loves us so much, that He died for us. He died so we could have everlasting life. Jesus bore the weight of sin on His shoulders, so we wouldn't have to. And know this, Jesus didn't sacrifice His life because we were worthy, it was to rescue us from unworthiness. We are flawed and broken, but that doesn't mean we can't still find joy and love in our lives.

It's time to realize that you have always been seen, heard, and loved by the highest of highs—God. This is your life, your journey, your adventure. You choose the path you want to walk down. Stop sacrificing your happiness by living in the past or in the words of someone else. Stop refusing help, stop thinking you don't need guidance, and just let God help you. Hear your Lord and Savior. God is calling you away from your comfort zone and into the unknown, but I promise you will find Him there. Sometimes it is at the end of something where you will find your new beginning. I know it's hard as our society has become accustomed to temporary things and maybe we've forgotten what we know about God. Find Him again. You can rise from anything with Him. Completely recreate yourself by hearing who He says you are. Use your experiences to drive you into the life you desire. It's your choice to make.

We are all going to experience a multitude of different seasons in life. My "in-between" experiences of high school were fascinating to say at the least. I changed a lot, grew in ways I didn't know possible, and began to love myself in a way I didn't know I could. Before entering my senior year at school, I decided to take a really big leap of faith and explore what the world had to offer by doing something that scared and excited me. I traveled to the Dominican Republic with an organization called Transform365 and spent a week working to rescue and redeem children and families from human trafficking. The experience completely broke my heart. It wrecked me and opened my mind to another meaning of pain. And at the same time, it put me back together. When I returned home, I felt weird. Everything seemed the same—my house, the people around me, the trees, the weather, the roads. Everything around me looked the same, but I felt like something was off. Then I realized that what was different was my heart.

This experience completely changed me. It caused me to become more grateful for my life. I am blessed beyond belief and have no reason to really complain. I feel so thankful to have grown up the way I did with Jesus at the forefront of our lives. The reason I share so much about this experience is because it was a life-altering moment for me. And I believe at any moment we have a choice to start again, readjust our attitudes, and surrender who we are and where we are going, to God. Going on this mission trip brought me a new perspective, mindset, and attitude. I realized how important it is for people to engage in adventure and travel. Age is irrelevant when it comes to traveling or serving abroad. Just see the world. I don't care how old or how young you are, it is so important that we see what life is like outside the tiny cocoons we make for ourselves. I encourage you to take a step outside your comfort zone and serve. Fully surrender yourself to what Jesus has placed on your heart to do. If you're looking for a sign to travel or serve, this is it, here's your sign. Be present in your life and through each experience. People will always have something to say about the choices you make, so you might as well make the one that YOU feel called to do.

So, between your goals, your next adventure, between becoming who you want to be, between seasons, it's scary and uncertain, but fall in love with the journey of growing. The "in-between" is a beautiful, sometimes awkward, and scary place, but it's when we grow, and it's when we find the truest form of grace.

Choose to immerse yourself wholeheartedly in giving to others and choose experiences that scare you. Listen deeply to others, understand people's pain and joy, be compassionate, and love. Find a way to accept the season you are in, but let it move you and grow you to the next chapter. Allow Jesus to wrap His graceful arms around you, and you and listen to what He is speaking into your heart to do. Be engaged.

I challenge you as you read these next chapters of letters from some very wise and faithful women, to really reflect and relate it to where you are at or maybe you know someone who needs to hear their words.

The next few chapters you will read are the letters I received for my 18th birthday. As I began to close the chapter of high school and my hometown, I needed encouragement, and inspiration for my next journey, college. It was time to start the wilderness phase of my life; picking a career path, saying goodbye to my friends I had known since pre-school, and it was time to learn the art of independence. Luckily, I had these women to guide me into this next season.

Chapter Thirteen

The Story of Seasons

Dear Kennedy,

Happy eighteenth birthday! I struggled with choosing one thing that I wish I had known at eighteen. There are a million things I wish I'd known. Another reason this was difficult is because you are so much more mature than I was at eighteen. Kennedy, you impress me.

I don't know if you remember this night in the Dominican Republic on our mission trip. We came back to the house after visiting with Keith and Amy Melugin, and you were in tears. You had realized the massive number of things you have taken for granted in your life. I looked at you and said, "Kennedy, you are a million miles ahead of most adults I know. Most people NEVER come to that realization." There were multiple times in our evening discussions that you gave all of us very important, Godly insight into the situations we had faced that day. God has big plans for you!

So, the one thing I wish someone told me when I was eighteen...

Listen to the voice of your Creator. The "world" is going to be wrong more times than you can imagine!

Marriage

My husband, Stan, and I went through some very difficult seasons in our marriage. The "world" told me for years that my marriage was too far gone. That there was no way we could make it work. Most of my friends and family members encouraged me to walk away. I had very few people in my life encouraging me to stay. During this time, I wavered back and forth between listening to the voices around me and listening to the voice of my Creator. This was one of the most difficult times of my life. There were many times I begged God to give me a way out. There was a season when every time Stan looked at me, all I saw was the disappointment and disgust he felt toward me. We were in a very bad place. Standing in the kitchen one morning, I looked at my husband with tears in my eyes and said, *"Thank you."*

With a very confused look on his face, he asked, *"For what?"*

I replied *"Thank you for pushing me away and treating me this way. Your actions have made me realize that God will provide ALL my needs. He is my friend, my comforter, my counselor, my healer, my provider, and even my husband because I don't have one right now."*

Through lots of counseling and putting God at the center of our lives, we began to heal. I wouldn't trade any of the pain and heartache for anything! I am so glad I chose to listen to the voice of God. God used the trials in our marriage to refine me with fire.

I have learned perseverance, commitment, and true intimacy. God used the most difficult times in our marriage and the mistakes we made along the way to draw me closer to Him. Our marriage is stronger than ever, and I am amazed, every day, that God has brought us to where we are today.

Career

I spent years building a clientele as a hairstylist. Six years into my career, a couple of friends and I opened our own salon. I considered my career a success. I loved my job! I loved all my clients and the opportunities I was given to speak to them about Jesus. I loved the people I worked with. I loved the flexibility. I felt like I was in a place that God wanted me to be.

At one point, I felt this overwhelming pull from the Spirit. I told my husband, "I don't know what is coming, but I feel like a big change is about to happen." One night after small group, a church leader mentioned that she was looking for someone to replace her as the kids' ministry director at Connections Community Church. After a few conversations and lots of prayer, I said yes. One of the conversations I had with God went something like this: "I will do this part-time as long as I don't ever have to stop being a hairstylist." I knew at that moment God was laughing.

For three years, I worked both jobs part-time. There were multiple times I felt God asking me to "retire" as a hairstylist, and I didn't listen. I had so many excuses. We couldn't live the same life we were living without my income. I would miss all my clients and the friends I had made in my career, and I would miss the validation it gave me. Three years later, I felt God telling me, again, to give up my career as a hairstylist. This time, I listened. He needed me to shift my focus. He needed me to create some space in my life. He needed me to simplify so that He could do a new work in me. He wanted to change me, heal me, restore me. He asked me to walk away from a lucrative business, owning my own hair salon, to work for a fraction of the money. In the eyes of the world, it looks crazy. In the world's eyes, it looks backward. In God's eyes, it was imperative. God opened my eyes to imperfections in me from my past, that needed to be addressed so I can be whole. I am so grateful that I listened to God's voice.

I listened to the world's voice for too long when it came to my marriage and my career, but God uses everything for His good for those that love Him (see Romans 8:28).

Love,

Kim

Chapter Fourteen

Be Authentic

My Dear Kennedy,

There are so many things I want to say to you, but one of the main ideas I want to share is to always strive to live the most authentic, unique, beautiful identity you have. You have an incredible spirit. We have shared so many stories and ideas about life with each other. I can see your uncanny level of discernment. This is a gift, Kennedy. Discernment is a powerful, unique gift from God, and it flows from you naturally. Use this to always pursue love, compassion, honesty, and passion. I pray as you begin a new chapter of your life that you will welcome each new adventure with a sense of openness, learning, and discovery. I am forty-two years old, and I still want to strive to learn about who I am and what decisions are best to express my identity.

As you look for opportunities in friendship, love, career, and family, always be open to learn but also always decide to enter these adventures based on your identity. If you can do things based on who you are and how you thrive, then your choices won't steer you wrong. Love people because it is in you to love deep. Show compassion because compassion is in your soul. Offer forgiveness because we are all broken and need a Savior. You were created with an amazing heart and spirit for adventure.

Please see toward these things in your life. Don't allow anything or anyone to keep you from fully being your whole self. Pursue life's challenges with passion and discernment. Handle people with kindness, exposing your loving heart. You are an angel to me, beautiful in ways that are so special to see. Your soul radiates from you, and it is breathtaking.

I love you sweet girl

Sarah

Chapter Fifteen

Ask for The Lord's Guidance

Kennedy,

What an incredible gift we have all been given to have you in our lives. The chance to watch you grow and develop with the Lord as your guide has been truly inspiring. I have many vivid pictures in my mind of chatting with your mom. She loved life and people and serving. I always enjoyed hearing about her next serving opportunity. In the past couple of years, I have witnessed you develop and follow in the same amazing footsteps! I admire how you carry yourself and how you treat people. I know from being a mom myself that she is SO proud of you, Kennedy!

I also see that your smile hides the pain and sacrifice of not being able to share these moments with your mom, and while none of us intend to replace your mom, please know that you are loved by all these women and that we have been blessed because of you in our lives. You are a real gift. I am so thankful for you.

As you embark on this new journey to college, first of all, I have no doubt that you will be successful. I also know that you will have struggles along the way. One of the things that I wish I had done more of at your age was to seek the Lord's guidance before making decisions. Sometimes we are quick to make decisions and forget to pray and ask for directions. I look back on many situations at that time of my life and realize that I was the one who chose the direction or path. I know that if I had prayed and put my trust in the Lord, the decision and outcome would have been different. Remember to seek first His wisdom and guidance. Pray, read your Bible, and seek out the godly family and friends in your life for the guidance and love you need. I read this verse this week and thought of you.

"Therefore whoever hears these sayings of Mine, and does them, I will liken him to a wise man who built his house on the rock: and the rain descended, the floods came, and the winds blew and beat on that house; and it did not fall, for it was founded on the rock." (Matthew 7:24-25, NKJV)

I know that you will have some great times as you head off to college and that you'll encounter some difficult situations as well. Just remember to continue to build your house on the rock. You are going to be amazing, and I can't wait to watch you begin on your next journey. Happy eighteenth birthday, Kennedy!

Love you,

Jenny

Chapter Sixteen

Establish Your Values

Dear Kennedy,

I wish I could send this letter back in time to myself when I turned eighteen and was headed off to college. I hope that it resonates with you at some point in your journey. I have gone back and forth and back and forth and back again about what I wanted to share with you tonight. I finally settled on an area in which I considered myself a bit of an expert back in the day...ugh...here goes...boys! My "expertise" comes from years of...umm...practice?!?! It comes from more dates than I can remember and more mistakes than I care to admit. I wish I had known how to navigate a few things twenty years ago. Here are my top three nuggets of advice when it comes to relationships with men. If you are into journaling, each of these would make a good writing prompt!

Purpose

I think it's important first to consider WHY we date. I'm sure we would all answer this question a bit differently, and I encourage you to spend some time contemplating this. Maybe it's to find a marriage partner or maybe it's not. Either way, it SHOULD be a time to learn about yourself. You are learning what you need and want as well as how you need to grow and change. Relationships should ALWAYS be helping you to grow, even when they hit rough spots. My husband and I are still growing after sixteen years of marriage, and I feel like we have so much to learn.

Dating for me in my late teens and twenties was solely for attention and companionship. I learned a lot about myself, but I was insecure and lonely—a perfect recipe for bad relationships. What ended up happening over and over was so predictable. A guy would show interest. I would be flattered. We would hang out at college parties or go out for a few days or a few months. I would get sick of him and move on. The pattern repeated itself over and over again with only a couple of guys that I actually cared about.

Sad, right? Yes, it was sad for all of us. I was so broken at the time and so far from God that I was using "relationships" to fill a void. I was not spiritually or emotionally healthy enough for my relationships to do what God had intended them to do. Stay connected to Christ first and always; only then can your relationships be healthy!

Values

This one is so very important. When you enter a relationship, it is important that you and your partner share common values. First, you must spend some time on yourself. Identify the characteristics you value more than anything else. Make a long list, then think and pray over this list until you have narrowed it down to a few things. I've included a bunch here to get you thinking. I have a feeling that once you identify your top values, you will begin to notice these things in your closest friendships, too. For example, if honesty is important to you, then there is a good chance that you have gravitated toward friendships with honest people. Trust the opinions of a select few of your closest, most trusted friends or family members when it comes to the guy you date; they have your best interest at heart.

Once you have put in the time to identify your personal core values, DON'T COMPROMISE on these things in your romantic relationships! If your top values don't matter or are not automatic to your partner, no amount of trying is going to make the relationship work, and you will continue to struggle. Please keep in touch on this one! I'd love to hear what you come up with.

Faith	Dependability	Loyalty	Commitment	Open-Mindedness
Consistency	Creativity	Efficiency	Innovation	Spirt of Adventure
Humor	Compassion	Optimism	Passion	Respect

Identity

Our identity has many components. First and foremost, it starts with who God says we are. Then things like our personalities, strengths, gifts, and passions define us further. When we enter a romantic relationship, this becomes part of who we are as well. But it is only a small piece. I'm sure we can all think of a friend who got so wrapped up in a relationship that we hardly saw her or spoke to her. Or maybe you've had a friend who completely changed her interests and how she spent her time because of the guy she was dating. This is not healthy.

When my husband and I started dating almost nineteen years ago, I knew something was different and I liked it. We were great together, but we also had our own interests and friend groups. We loved being together but also respected the friendships that we had before we were a couple. Our early relationships were free of jealousy and neediness that I had experienced with other guys, and it was great! A healthy relationship should always make us better and stronger. Our partner needs to be able to support, encourage, and challenge us, and we need to be able to do the same for him. Remember also that there are some seasons in which it is best for us to be alone. In times of being alone, we are often closest to God. I REALLY wish I had embraced this in my younger years.

I was in a much different place in my faith than I think you are now. I think you know that the most important part of walking this path is knowing that our Lord, Jesus Christ, wants a deep, personal relationship with you. If you stay rooted in that one thing alone, your other relationships will continue to thrive.

I love you more than you know and will continue to pray for you often. If you ever have a boys-are-stupid-and-I-need-my-momma moment, you have my number, and I would be honored to listen and talk through it. Call me.

XOXO

Lindsey

Chapter Seventeen

Do Not Be Afraid

Dear Kennedy,
Happy eighteenth birthday!

I am beyond blessed to be connected to you. Although our personal connection came later in your life, I always loved all the stories about you from your mom. You were such a gift to her. There are many lessons I learned from my teenage self as I grew older...and continue to learn today. Your mom always called me a "stubborn fixer of everyone else's problems" and "Amanda who can handle it all." I always laughed when she said this and found it ironic because she was the exact same way! Right, Kennedy?! I see that a bit in you.

One major lesson I have learned in my life that has really saved me, especially lately, is to ask for help. It is really hard to do, and I practice every day. No one can know it all, know how to do it all, or do it all themselves. A mentor of mine said, "It is a strength to ask for help." It took a long time for me to realize how true those words are. Help comes in many forms—prayers, having someone come alongside you, physical help, monetary help, counseling, someone seeing something in you that you don't or can't see in yourself, and more. I know that every person at this table, as well as many more not at this table, would be happy to help anytime you need it. You must do the hardest part though. You have to ask.

One more lesson I have learned is that relationships matter. In fact, relationships help you in many ways. I think this is something you already know, but it is important to build relationships and grow them in all aspects of life—spiritual, personal, social, professional, and of course familial. Relationships help you stay strong, keep you connected to others, foster your growth, and even help get you advancements in careers. But relationships are hard sometimes too. It is important to take time to affirm people you are connected to (something you are already good at it), and it is important to say "I'm sorry" when it is necessary.

Forgiveness is a big part of relationships. It is an absolute. We are all human and far from perfect, hence, forgiveness needs to happen often with each other and from God. Always forgive others, and of course, always forgive yourself. As you already know in your young life, life is too short to not love and forgive every day. Above all else, remember that God has a plan for you and live each day just as you do now, with joy, love, and the strength He has given you. I am so proud of you and the woman you have become. You are a shining light in a sometimes-dark world for your family, friends, and anyone who knows you. Continue shining your light that God blesses you with each day!

Love,

Amanda

Chapter Eighteen

Joy in The Journey

Dear Kennedy,

Happy eighteenth birthday! It's hard to believe it has been two years since we celebrated your previous milestone, your sixteenth birthday! With that said, you are probably already figuring out that in life the days seem to pass slowly but years fly by! How exciting it is to stand at these crossroads and look back on all the experiences and people that have shaped you thus far and look forward to a future that is laid out before you like an open road. How blessed I am (and I know the other ladies here feel the same) to be part of your journey. We know and believe that God has a wonderful future planned out because He cares so deeply for you, and we all look forward to seeing His path unfold in your life.

I stand here with you today filled with joy and hope as I gaze into your future, from my vantage point. How blessed I am to be able to share what I've learned and pass that on to you with the hope it gives you wisdom and direction. My heart's desire is that you experience life in all its fullness because that's what Jesus died to give us as He says Himself in John 10:10. I have learned that there are no shortcuts to a full, abundant life, but there are straight roads that will take you there more quickly as you apply God's Word and wisdom to your heart and situations. His Word will help you avoid the pitfalls and potholes and give you the strength to climb up the hills and over the hurdles that are common to us all as we journey through life.

You are ready to take the next step down a new road, and it is exciting. I want to encourage you to take it all in! Accept everything this moment has to offer you—learn from the lessons you've received up to this point and listen to the people God has placed in your path. Both are here to prepare you to take that next step. This is how we learn and grow. Life is constantly moving and changing, but in that activity, I challenge you to find the stillness. It's a delicate balance, but if you can learn to be present without wishing the moment away to the future, you will find beauty and blessing in each moment and stage of life.

I remember the anticipation I felt walking into my dorm room for the first time and thinking, I can't wait to meet new people and perhaps find a new boyfriend! Well, I met my boyfriend the day my parents dropped me off, and that led to I can't wait to get married! Then I got married and couldn't wait to have a baby, and then I couldn't wait until my children went to school, and now, looking back, I can see that I kept looking ahead when I should have been looking around. I kept anticipating the "next thing" instead of looking at the "present thing" that was right in front of me and finding joy and blessing right where I was.

So, I encourage you to find joy in your journey no matter what step you are on by choosing to look for the positive in each situation and finding something every day to be thankful for.

Gratitude helps us see what there is, instead of what there is not, and turns what we have into enough. There will be days when you'll find so many things to be thankful for, and there will be days that you'll have to look a little harder. But every day there is something. Focus on the positive, the blessings and goodness of God each day, and you will be protected from the bitterness that can creep in and harden your heart.

Look to Him every day and thank Him for His blessings...and rest assured in Psalm 73:24, *"He will keep guiding you with His counsel and leading you toward a glorious destiny!"*

God Bless You!

Love,

Kristen

Chapter Nineteen

Life Is About Dancing in The Rain

Dear Kennedy,

Adapt, don't accept.

Some things in life allow no do-overs; make careful choices.

There is no such thing as it can't be done.

Life is short, no matter how old you are.

You don't have to kneel to pray.

Don't put off your feelings...communicate with someone about them!

The best acts of kindness are those known only to you and the recipient.

Don't sweat the small things; they don't matter.

Love like your life depends on it; it does!

At your age, retirement may seem a hundred years away, but it is not. Start saving now.

Marriage is not always fifty-fifty.

"I challenge you to be a dreamer, I challenge you to be doers and let us make the greatest place in the world even better."— Brian Schweitzer, former governor of Montana

Time you enjoy wasting is not wasted time.

Don't spend more than you earn; it leads to chaos and heartache.

We all need a hug day, even if it is from ourselves.

Men and women are diametrically different. Take time to learn the differences.

In a relationship, always make time for each other no matter what.

"In the book of life, the answers are not in the back."—Charlie Brown/Charles M. Schultz

Love,

Nancy

Chapter Twenty

Delay Gratification and Live Generously

Dearest Kennedy,

On this special day celebrating your first day officially in the adult world, my topics of focus are about delayed gratification and sharing lessons learned on my journey with money in an effort to help you avoid the same mistakes I made. And more importantly, I want to share what God says about money, so you have a foundational knowledge before leaving for college this fall.

Achieving success usually comes down to choosing the pain of discipline over the ease of distraction. And that's exactly what delayed gratification is all about. Studies show that delayed gratification is one of the most effective personal traits of successful people. People who learn how to manage their needs to be satisfied in the moment thrive more in their careers, relationships, health, and finances than people who give in to it. Being able to delay satisfaction isn't the easiest skill to acquire. It involves feeling dissatisfied, which is why it seems impossible for people who haven't learned to control their impulses. Choosing to have something now might feel good but making the effort to have discipline and manage your impulses can result in bigger or better rewards in the future. Over time, delaying gratification will improve your self-control and ultimately help you achieve your long-term goals faster.

The numbers don't lie. The average college student graduates with nearly $30,000 in student loan debt. More than 40 million Americans currently have student loans—a larger number than the entire population of more than 190 countries, including Canada, Poland, and Australia.

The problem is that the younger generations in America have been taught that debt is OK, and those statistics reflect that. Most students don't know the basics about money—why debt is bad, why saving matters, and how to budget.

Debt is Not OK

Student loans, car payments, credit cards—they're a way of life for most people. You will probably hear all about "good debt versus bad debt" at some point. But there's no such thing. My mistake was listening to this lie in my early years of college when I was approached about "establishing my credit" and was offered a free T-shirt or pizza or both if I signed up for a credit card. Not a good decision for a person already working to pay for college and other expenses. All debt is bad debt. It complicates your life, adds unneeded stress, and places a huge obstacle in your path as soon as you graduate college.

Lesson 1: Make sure to avoid debt at all costs!

"The rich rule over the poor, and the borrower is slave to the lender" (Proverbs 22:7, NIV).

"Owe nothing to anyone except to love one another; for he who loves his neighbor has fulfilled the law" (Romans 13:8, NASB).

"The wicked borrows and does not pay back, But the righteous is gracious and gives" (Psalm 37:21, NASB).

You Won't Build Wealth Without a Budget

As much as I know your heart for serving and wanting to give generously, I know that your future involves building wealth so you can give freely and often to help others in need. A budget is your plan and way to get there. In his book 2 *The Total Money Makeover*, author Dave Ramsey wrote, "*John Maxwell has the best quote on budgeting I have ever heard... A budget is people telling their money where to go instead of wondering where it went.*" A budget will help you avoid overspending on things like pizza, lattes, and late-night movies while you're away at college.

Lesson 2: Use an app like Dave Ramsey's EveryDollar to track your budget and stick with it. Get creative on how you save money and remember that money is finite. When it is gone, it's gone.

"Make sure that your character is free from the love of money, being content with what you have; for He Himself has said, "I WILL NEVER DESERT YOU, NOR WILL I EVER FORSAKE YOU (Hebrews 13:5, NASB).

You Can Be a Student Without a Loan

It's possible. I promise! Scholarships, grants, and an old-fashioned job are great ways to avoid having another twenty-two-year-old who graduates with debt. I know after the last few months, that you are already well on your way to not being in debt from all the scholarship applications you have spent time writing and the hard work you have put in ahead of time to receive them. There are jobs and other sensible ways you can earn money in college and still maintain your studies. For you, I think about you using your basketball talents and being a referee at youth basketball games or using your knowledge of the Bible in leading a college Bible study or using your leadership skills and influence in being a residence hall adviser. The ideas are endless!

Lesson 3: It is possible to graduate from college without student loans or other debt. Trust me, you do not want to spend ten to fifteen years paying off student loans or any other kind of loan. You would much rather be using that monthly payment to live your fullest life ever and give generously!

"But seek first his kingdom and his righteousness, and all these things will be given to you as well" (Matthew 6:33, NIV).

Financial debt is a form of slavery. (See Proverbs 22:7 and Deuteronomy 28:43-44.)

Live Generously

Give. Give. Give. You simply can't go wrong with giving, because that's what God called us to do. Something changes in your spirit when you become a giver. You focus less on yourself and see the needs of others more. I know you have already learned the lesson and power of giving from your mom, and I have seen that natural gift in you on our mission trip and in daily life. Now go out and live your mom's legacy in loving and giving to others.

Lesson 4: Giving doesn't always have to mean money. It can also mean giving your time, talents, resources, energy, and prayers.

"Such is the fate of all who are greedy for money; it robs them of life."

—Proverbs 1:19, NLT

"Those who love money will never have enough. How meaningless to think that wealth brings true happiness!"

—Ecclesiastes 5:10, NLT

"Don't love money; be satisfied with what you have. For God has said, "I will never fail you. I will never abandon you."

—Hebrews 13:5, NLT

"No one can serve two masters; for either he will hate the one and love the other, or he will be devoted to one and despise the other. You cannot serve God and wealth."

—Matthew 6:24, NASB

"Whoever loves money never has enough; whoever loves wealth is never satisfied with their income. This too is meaningless."

—Ecclesiastes 5:10, NIV

Delaying gratification isn't a new concept. Back in 300 BC, Aristotle saw that the reason so many people were unhappy was that they confused pleasure for true happiness. True happiness, according to Aristotle, is about developing habits and surrounding yourself with people who grow your soul. This allows you to move toward your greatest potential. True happiness entails delaying pleasure, putting in the time, discipline, and patience instead of feeling good now. A life of purpose, aligned with the seeking of true happiness, creates real joy. It keeps your happiness meter pretty steady throughout your life.

As you head into what I like to call the "wilderness phase" of your life, take time to really get to know yourself fully. It's OK to be alone in quiet solitude on occasion. This helps you hear God and His plans for your life.

I wish you joy, gratitude, purpose, and love today, in the next phase of your life journey, and always.

Love you,

Kristin

Chapter Twenty-One

Forever Friends

After my 18th birthday, I realized how important it was for me to truly be surrounded by women who support, encourage, and challenge me. My mother had these people in her life, and those people who were there for her, are now there for me. I am surrounded by love and strength from numerous people. I believe that God created us for genuine friendship. God created us to be connected, to love, and to help one another. *Proverbs 17:17 states, "A friend loves at all times."* When I think about these characteristics of a friend, two women specifically stick out, Laura and Tammie.

It was the day after my fourteenth birthday party, and I all I wanted that year was to go see my mother in the hospital. I woke up in the morning and got ready quickly. I began to walk down the steps and passed my dad.

"Are we going to see Mom soon?" I questioned.

No answer.

I thought maybe he was tired or just sad, but nothing could have possibly prepared me for what has going to happen next. Minutes later my dad came back down the stairs as I sat in the living room crouched in our black rocking chair. My dad began to speak slowly.

"Kennedy, Pastor Dave and I prayed over the phone early this morning about Mom. Kennedy, Mom didn't make it. She's in a better place..."

He talked a little bit more, but I couldn't hear, my heart was beating too loudly. I felt my stomachache turn as if I was about to puke. My palms became sweaty. The room was spinning.

This couldn't be real.

My younger brother walked into the room; his eyes were already swollen from crying. We hugged for a moment, and then I found my way back to my bedroom.

There is nothing in this world can possibly prepare you for losing someone you love. No matter how long someone is sick, or in the hospital. No matter how much you think about it or try to adapt in your head. Nothing. There is nothing that can help you cope when you hear that horrible, heart wrenching, news.

Do you know that feeling of sadness you get in the pit of your stomach? The feeling of utter despair, confusion, and pain. A million moments with my mother flashed through my head, and then it all went numb. Time seemed to be moving so slowly, I watched the clock on my phone minute by minute, nothing seemed real. Then, I heard two voices downstairs, and sure enough, it was them, Laura and Tammie.

These two women had been a part of my life since I was seven years old. Our families were brought together because my older brother played baseball with their sons from the time they started with Tee-ball. Laura and Tammie were always fun and happy, and they loved me like one of their own. They were two of my mother's best friends.

But, when my mom first began to get "sick," she pushed them out of her life. It was heartbreaking—for my mom and for them. No one could really understand what my mom was feeling or going through, and she was so good at hiding her pain. As we know, God didn't intend for us to live alone. We require connection, love, relationships, and intimacy. It was when my mom pushed people out, she began to lose her sense of self and well-being.

Laura and Tammie shared experiences with me no one can really understand. They, too, watched my mother become sicker and sicker, they watched her withdrawal socially, her body thin, and moods change. They saw the two different "Trish" personalities just as closely as I did.

The two different Trish's was a real and scary experience for me. For a while the doctors thought she had bipolar disorder, and some really had no idea what was going on. I realize now why and how this was happening. My mother's body was changing because of her anorexia, alcohol abuse, lack of sleep, stress, and depression. The chemical balances in her brain were literally altering. Her failing liver had a ripple effect, causing a plethora of issues in her body. Aside from her medical/mental problems, I want to focus on the friendship Laura and Tammie created with my mother.

After losing my mom, my idea of friendship changed, and I began to look at friendships differently. I've come to value honesty, loyalty, support, and love—more of what really matters in life. I am tired of surface level, fake friendships but instead look to cultivate authenticity and true joy between people. I also remember that life isn't meant to be taken so seriously all the time, and friendships are meant to be fun. We need to engage in adventure, lots of laughter, smiles, and exhilarating experiences. We need to relish friendships that teach us to enjoy the ride and that happiness is not a destination, but more of a journey. And we need friendships that teach us to embrace not only those great moments in life but the moments of hardship, weakness, and vulnerability too. This was the type of friendship my mother had with Laura and Tammie.

After my mother died, these two women never gave up on me. I spent countless hours with them crying, laughing, and remembering all the beautiful times we shared with her. They were the first responders the day of my mom's death, along with my Aunt Julie, Aunt Marissa and Uncle Gordy, my grandparents, and even a few of my cousins, I was blessed with a wonderful support system to say the least. But when I think about Laura and Tammie showing up at my house the day my mother died, it was different. They weren't family, but they cared for me as if I was. They chose to be there for my whole family. They chose to love me through my pain. So, when I think about the friendship my mom had with those two women, I remember the story of the prodigal son. You might be trying to connect the dots in your head, but here is why:

If you haven't heard of it, the story of the prodigal son is the story of a rebellious son who rejects his father's upbringing. This son is seemingly prideful, arrogant, and strong-willed. The son leaves home and travels to a faraway land, where he lives a wildlife of adventure and squanders everything of value (literally and symbolically). Not until he's confronted with failure and despair does, he returns home, repentant and willing to do anything to win back his father's favor. To his surprise, and the surprise of others, he's welcomed, without question, into his father's loving and forgiving arms. No amount of time, no amount of money, and no amount of rebellion could get in the way of the father's patience and unconditional love for his son.

"For this son of mine was dead and is alive again; he was lost and is found" (Luke 15:24, NIV).

Of course, the awesome message of this parable is that God is patient and gracious with all His children. He is willing to welcome each of us home into His loving and forgiving arms.

But how does this connect to Laura and Tammie?

It did not matter how hard my mother pushed them away. Or the feelings that were hurt between them. At the end of it all, there was forgiveness, grace, and love. My mother, Laura, and Tammie have had their fair share of ups and downs, but at the end of the day, they chose to love each other. They are forever friends. To this day, they continue to support my whole family. They embody so beautifully the love Jesus has for each and every one of us. They treated me just as they did my mother, it didn't matter how far I ran from them, how long we went without talking, Tammie and Laura refused to give up on me. Mistakes and all, they loved deeply.

It doesn't matter how far you run from Jesus, because the moment you decide to turn back, Jesus is waiting with open arms.

I can't even begin to thank the people who were there for me when I lost my mom. The broad range of people; strangers to teachers to close friends, so many showed the true light of Jesus. The acts of compassion, kindness, and love I received during the most painful time in my life may be beyond my ability to ever repay. From my closest friends to people I hardly knew, I was truly cared for. The passing of my mother has brought me closer to so many people, and without them, I would not be where I am today. Thank you to everyone who was there for me when I felt my loneliest, thank you for the ongoing support, encouragement, and love you have given.

Chapter Twenty-Two

Forgiving the Bottle

Bitterness is the enemy of love because it makes you unforgiving and unwilling to give love unconditionally. I was very bitter; I still am in some ways. I was angry with my mother and couldn't forgive her for not asking for help. And I was angry with her family and unforgiving toward them. My dad and siblings had a falling out with my mom's sister when we first lost my mom. Tensions were high, no one could really understand why or how my mom died, and all our hearts missed my mom. I have realized that death can bring out the best and worst in families.

What I have learned, through my mom's childhood experiences, my own endeavors, and those around me is this: YOU are responsible for your life. You can't keep blaming others for your own dysfunction. You and only you are responsible for every decision and choice you make. This doesn't mean my mom wasn't sick, but this does mean she had a choice, and sometimes, we make the wrong ones, and that's just life.

Most of us in some way grow up with a little bit of dysfunction in their household, it's normal. My grandparents both had their quirks, and dealt with some health issues, mental and physical, this took a toll on my mom. If there is one thing my mom and I have in common from our childhoods, it's the presence of alcohol, and the stubbornness of family members never asking for help. My grandfather, who I love dearly, never received the help my mother thought he should have received, he was a Vietnam war veteran, a medic, who dealt with PTSD. In 2019, I lost my papa due to health complications. I find peace in knowing that he finally gets to be with his daughter again and all the brokenness and hurt has been wiped clean. It makes sense why my mother never reached out for help, because my grandfather seemed to be the same way. And I guess that trait shows up in me somewhat, too.

Why do we always wait until it's too late? It seems as if so, many people try to "tough it out" or "be strong", and not ask for help. We seem to hold grudges to "prove a point", but honestly what's the point of not forgiving someone? Haven't we learned by now that we can lose anyone at any moment. I believe that asking for help, forgiving people, and asking for forgiveness is the bravest move you can make in life.

After my papa passed, it brought up again all the treacherous feelings of loss. Grief is confusing and sometimes makes us do out-of-the-ordinary things. Losing the people, the ones we hold closest to our hearts, is confusing and terrifying. When I look at the household my mother grew up in, I see a lot of dysfunction. It's the same with a lot of people. There was dysfunction in my own home. Every family has it. I look at my grandparents, my parents, friends' families, and friends, and I see the pain and damage that has been caused by addictions, substance abuse, mental diseases, etc. but through all those fractures, I see Jesus.

Being in college, I have learned the fine lines between alcohol, and how easily it can become destructive. I've heard the broad range of sayings, "alcohol tastes better than tears" or "If you can't be happy at least you can be drunk" or "I'm sorry liver!" Don't get me wrong, I don't hate alcohol, I don't hate drinking, I just hate how it can completely change, and hurt a person, and even destroy relationships among friends and family.

My mom was a silent and functioning alcoholic. An addiction is a family disease, one person may use, but the whole family suffers. So, I don't hate alcohol, but I hate what it can do to people. I don't hate drinking; I hate when it's abused.

Everyone in life battles something internally whether we realize it or not. It's been one of the biggest realizations for me that even "grown-ups," like my grandparents and parents or aunts and uncles, brothers, or mentors, have some sort of mental obstacle.

Growing up, my mother faced some tough situations that I don't necessarily know the depth of but can infer they cut her deep because of her coping mechanisms. She informed my dad before they got married about the sexual trauma that she had endured, along with other situations that had stuck with her. She explained to him the depth of her anorexia, and mental issues. Sometimes I feel like my mom didn't even have a chance of living a full and long life. I wish I could change the cards she was dealt, but I know that thinking is wrong, and I know she thinks that, too. She'd probably tell me,

"Kennedy, there are children born every day addicted to drugs because of their mothers. There are people who will never go as far as I've gone in life just because of where they are born geographically. There are people who will never experience the type of love I have. Those kids are the ones who seem to not even have a chance. I made a few of wrong choices, but those mistakes don't define me, I lived a wonderful life."

She would have something along those lines. But she would have also lectured me about how we are all given the same 24 hours. Each day, no matter your ethnicity, skin color, religious views, popularity, background, social status, pain that you have felt, wrongdoings, or sins, you are given the same 24 hours. Many things in life are unfair, and unequal, but everyone gets the same 24 hours. It's what we do with those hours that sets us apart and into the life we want, our choices are the most powerful tool we have.

My parents always drank casually on the weekends, alcohol consumption was just a part of their lives. I never thought anything of it. Weekdays were filled with sporting events, school, and work. The weekends, after more sporting events, would be time spent with friends at the pool or small get-togethers— always involving alcohol. Then on Sundays, we would go to church, and it was family day. To be honest, in so many ways I seemed to have had it perfect. My parents were happy, had great jobs, in love with each other, and in love with their children.

Somewhere along this beautiful life, my mom became very lost. The domino effect began, it seems like everything that could have gone wrong, went wrong. She had to quit the job she loved at the church due to financial issues, and it was devastating for her. My mom got a new job at Western Michigan University, but it was then that her overwhelming responsibilities, travel, and work deadlines consumed her life. During this chaos, her parents got a divorce, and my mom began to spiral out of control. You could see the exhaustion in her eyes and how much she missed spending time at home, and then it happened. She resorted back to her old coping habits. She stopped eating right and turned to drinking. The first time she was admitted into the hospital, the psych ward, I was in sixth grade, and from then on life was an absolute roller coaster.

There are many disorders associated with alcoholism. Conduct disorder, personality disorders antisocial personality, anxiety, eating disorders, and depression. In some way, shape, or form, my mom battled all of these. I previously mentioned part of her background, in her college years she was bulimic, eating larger quantities of food and then puking what she ate back up. Eventually this bulimia turned to anorexia, she completely stopped eating. When my mother and father's relationship got serious, she told him that she didn't believe her body was strong enough to have kids. But my dad and God changed that for her, God gave her 3 beautiful children, and she became the worlds most wonderful mom.

I hear stories about how my mom was the healthiest; mentally, physically, and spiritually when she was pregnant. She was incredible, she defied the odds.

When I was in middle school and the unhealthy coping came back, it left a scar so deep that I would carry it with me for the rest of my life. I had never known she had these issues until my dad had no choice but to tell me when she was hospitalized. The last few years of her life, there would be moments I would look her in the eyes and have no idea who the woman looking back at me was. It hurt. It was scary. And now it just seems to be so baffling. I constantly question what drives a person to be like this? Why do so many become trapped in the disease of addiction?

It was hard to comprehend that my mom was addicted to the numbing of alcohol, and it was hard to understand that she felt so out of control of her life, that she had to drastically control the food she ate. After witnessing my mother and other family members struggle with the trap of addiction, the thought that I might turn to alcohol or unhealthy eating habits to cope with difficult times in my life is unnerving, but my awareness of this issue will guide me to make the right choices. The first step to overcoming these matters is awareness. For me, a newly found awareness was also the beginning of a journey toward forgiveness. But I never forgave my mom until 2018—four years after she died.

Sometimes when someone is suffering internally, that suffering can spill over onto other people. My mom didn't need people getting angry at her or deciding whether she was right or wrong. She needed help. She never properly received it. It pains me to think about how hard my dad tried to get her what she needed. But as the old saying goes, you can lead a horse to water, but you can't make it drink. I made the mistake of acting out of anger instead of compassion. This caused me to feel ashamed, and I struggled with forgiving myself for holding a grudge against her and not being able to understand the complications of what was going on.

Forgiving people can be hard. Forgiving yourself can be even harder. Sometimes I used to think that God could never possibly forgive me, yet He still does. We ultimately get to make the choice to forgive people, to forgive ourselves, and to ask for forgiveness. We may not be able to wipe away the pain someone has caused us, but we can choose to move forward. We can find a way to let go of bitterness, anger, any desire for revenge, and our struggle to understand why everything happens the way it does. Instead, we can trust in God, His judgment, and His plan. Ultimately, it is NOT our job to judge people, or control them, it's our job to forgive, love, and encourage.

Some days when I struggled with forgiving someone, I would think back to when I was little and my parents would say, *"God is always watching!"* to prevent me from lying or eating candy when I wasn't supposed to. But the thing is that now, I don't want to know that God is just watching, I want Him to be involved in how everything plays out. I want Him to give me the sense of revenge for the hurt some people have given me. I think *God, please do something to make this person feel what I am feeling.* Instead, I know I should be praying for that person, for my heart, and be treating those people how God treats me, that means with love and forgiveness. When we want to solve the situation, we should give it up to God, let him take control of our hearts, and breathe.

When we want God to help us truly forgive someone to understand that He is in charge of the situation, we must continually pursue the word of our Lord. This whole forgiveness thing can be even tougher for some of us because we seem to be obsessed with the idea of being in complete control. We struggle to let go of a situation and admit that, in fact, we have absolutely no control of the ending. That's where our downfall is because sometimes, we try to compensate for this lack of control by choosing whether to forgive someone. Although when we choose to live like Jesus, we choose the path of forgiveness. That means we choose to be forgiven and to forgive.

I believe that forgiveness is power. Occasionally, we need forgiveness and grace just to breathe again. When we forgive another, our forgiveness may or may not affect that person's well-being, but our forgiveness will affect us. Forgiving someone is never about letting that person off the hook for their actions; instead, it's essentially about freeing ourselves of the negative energy and soul-crushing situations that bind us to them. It's about giving the situation to our God who can handle it—and handle it the right way and in the best way. His way.

It is in forgiveness that we can find a new beginning. My dad bought me a brand-new CSB She Reads Truth Bible for Christmas in 2018. I decided that it was time for me to finally crack it open and get to some reading. It had been a rough season in my life. I had been neglecting my faith altogether. It was the holiday season and I all I could think about was yet another year without mom here, and it still didn't seem right. I became envious and jealous of all the families who got to spend their Christmas together. And let's just be real, moms have a special way of making Christmas feel magical in a sense. I felt like the magic was lost that year. Sure, I still found moments of bliss with my brothers, and seeing my father's smile always warms my heart. I enjoyed giving gifts to family and eating endless amounts of food. But a piece was missing.

When I opened my new Bible, I decided to pray before reading anything. Praying first is something I am slowly getting in the habit of doing because reading the Bible prayerfully always helps me see what Jesus wants me to see. I prayed that God would lead me to what I needed to read. I prayed for forgiveness and clarity.

I prayed that I could, just for once, hear Him. I felt very lost and sad. Tears filled my eyes, and I could feel my heart sink, and then the words whispered through my mind, "Genesis is a book of beginnings."

I quickly opened the bible. You're probably like, Yeah, OK, Kennedy, everyone knows that, and everyone has read that, not super insightful. But my heart sank, I had heard the words probably thousands of times in my life, but this time those words resonated with me differently. I realized that at any moment we have an opportunity to begin again. But more importantly, God created me, my mother, and knew that someday I would be in this exact moment. I realized that at any time, I can find a new beginning. Reading the book of genesis that day taught me that:

1. God keeps his promises.

2. Holding onto anger only hurts us.

3. You reap what you sow.

How is it that we as humans still don't rely on the power of Jesus Christ? The fact is that we can be wiped completely clean and start anew in His name every single day. **At any moment, we can choose to begin again.** We can make decisions to completely turn our life around and run back to Him. We were given this power of free will. We are all able to walk hand in hand with God. Every single one of us. We can fully feel forgiveness and grace. Learning to put our purpose, identity, and life in Him can be one of the most difficult things we wrestle with as humans. But the seasons of my life when I've wholeheartedly put myself on God's hands have been some of the most beautiful, eye-opening, and strengthening seasons of my life. Those seasons were ones where my eyes saw the best in people, my heart forgave the worst, my mind forgot the bad, and my soul never lost sight of God.

I encourage you down the path of redemption and grace. Where we can choose to start again. We can have a new beginning in His goodness. Approach God's Word, read it, engage in it, apply it, and be doers of His word. You are meant to hear it, and you are meant to reflect it. You are good enough. You are worthy. You have a story to tell that just might change the perspective and mindset of someone else. You have no idea of your capabilities until you learn to just let go. Let God choose the new beginning our Savior has to offer through His salvation and forgiveness.

We can't change people. We aren't supposed to. We can love them for where they are at, addiction and all. We can be an example, we can be doers of His word, lovers, forgivers, encouragers, and fighters.

We can forgive ourselves and allow it to be a form of self-care. Sometimes we must look at our failures and disappointments right in the eyes and choose to let them go. Forgive yourself for not knowing better at the time, for giving away your power, for your past behaviors and actions. Some people even need to forgive themselves for survival patterns and traits picked up while enduring trauma.

I think our society has an immense problem with the thought of giving up and into God. We have become accustomed to the temporary pleasures. We seem to have forgotten what we know about God.

- He created this entire earth and every soul on it.

- He created the stars and the universe.

- He knows you better than you know yourself.

- He sees you as worthy.

- He sees you as forgiven.

- He offers us the ability to completely start again with Him.

I had to choose to forgive the bottle my mom clung to so tightly. I had to choose to forgive how she chose to escape her trauma. And it was in that forgiveness, I found a new beginning.

Chapter Twenty-Three

The Truths About Love

I sat motionless with tears streaming down my face. I could feel my eyes getting puffier by the minute. I remember thinking, *why am I crying!? Get it together Kennedy!* But, I couldn't. I sat on the bathroom floor of my college dorm trying to muffle my cries. My phone buzzed, I grabbed it quickly, it was a text from my best friend in the other room, the text read:

Are you okay? I love you.

I cracked a smile; I knew I was blessed with incredible friends. As I sat there, I began thinking how on earth are we as women supposed to handle hormones and periods? You might be laughing, and I am sure my brothers read this part and laughed, too. I tend to be dramatic sometimes, but I felt as if I had let love, relationships, and friendships take me to a place where I felt so alone. I was overthinking, overanalyzing, and stressing out over every little detail of my life. I wished more than anything in that moment to send one text, call one time, have one facetime, anything just to hear what my mother's advice would be. Then I remembered I couldn't talk to her, only making my sadness deepen.

I could hear my John Mayer music echoing in the background, I felt a tear glide down by face and watched it hit the ground. I listened closer to the music,

"I hate to see you cry

Laying there in that position

There are things you need to hear

So, turn off your tears and listen

Pain throws your heart to the ground

Love turns the whole thing around

No, it won't all go the way, it should

But I know the heart of life is good

You know it's nothing new

Bad news never had good timing

But then the circle of your friends

Will defend the silver lining"

AM I IN A MOVIE??? I smiled at myself and thought, *quit being such a drama queen!* I evaluated what was going and decided to pray and count my blessings. It didn't heal of my pain in that moment, but I felt better.

I realize now that having breakdowns occasionally, is normal. Life, emotions, friendships, love, and relationships can be hard to navigate. In these moments of total vulnerability, I decided to journal, and from there I drew a conclusion. I am not too emotional. I am not too sensitive. I realized that our hearts are at war with fighting our emotions and listening to what God is whispering to us. If you have ever felt like you were emotionally weak, I want you to know that I don't think you are. I think you have a huge heart that feels the energies of others deeply, and I believe you care intensely, and you are kind. I hope you know that God loves us so much, he feels our pain when we hurt, and he wants so badly to take care of us; let Him.

Isn't love a strange thing? I believe there are different kinds and types of love, and we experience all these kinds throughout our time here on earth. If you haven't noticed by now, my book is full of the word LOVE. There is probably no subject ever discussed among us that is more captivating and more mysterious than love. But it's because I believe we are driven by love and we are driven to love.

My mother was a prolific reader, she had shelves and boxes absolutely filled with books of all different genres. I love reading the books she's read because I can see the places, she's highlighted, noted, and underlined. One of the books she read was Soul Cravings by Erwin Raphael McManus. A passage she had underlined stood out to me. It read:

"When love does not come to you, it breaks your heart, but when you do not give love away, it hardens your heart. One thing stranger than our need to be loved is our need to love, which

again leads me to my conspiracy theory: We are designed for love...

Inside all of us is an intrinsic need to belong... It as if each of us is searching for a love we have lost."

We are relational people because we serve a relational God. We love, because our God first loved us. Our hearts long for love, because our creator is love.

By now, you understand that when my mom was sick, she would have these "moments." The moments were products of extreme exhaustion, alcohol consumption, her eating disorder, and stress. In these moments I witnessed someone who was not my real mom but instead a very confused, disoriented, lost woman. She would hallucinate and accuse people—especially my dad and, of course, her children—of things that never happened.

One of these moments happened during the summer before I began the seventh grade. My mom was exhausted and stayed home from work that day (we all understood she needed the sleep more than anything). My dad left for work, and my brother Karson went to the neighbor's house. Parker, my other brother, went off to his girlfriend's house. I decided to go hang out with my friend Sabrina. I hopped on my bike and off I went. Two hours later my little red flip phone began to vibrate in my pocket.

When I saw MOM CELL PHONE highlighted across the screen, my heart dropped; I knew something bad was coming. But it wasn't the kind of "uh-oh" feeling a normal teenage girl should feel. It wasn't that classic getting in trouble because I didn't tell her where I was going or that I needed to head home for lunch. No, I knew it was going to be one of her moments.

"Kennedy, you need to come home this instant!" she was hysterical. *"There are people in the house! Please, Kennedy, come home now."*

I lied to Sabrina and told her that my mom had some chores around the house I needed to do, and I had to head home. I honestly have never ridden a bike as fast as I did that day—or seen anyone else ride so fast. I tried to stay calm as I repeatedly called my dad and older brother.

I pulled into the driveway and could see my mother in the garage pointing and talking as if someone was in there with her. I was nervous and felt the tears begin well up in my eyes.

"Mom let's go inside. Please!"

She proceeded to name the people in front of her and explain what they were doing there and how it was all just a misunderstanding. She told me there were vampires. Yes, vampires. They were her normal go-to people when she hallucinated, but she believed what she saw was real. It was terrifying for me to have her think there were people in front of her when clearly no one was there.

We walked inside as she continued to babble on hysterically. In my kitchen, all the lights were off, and on the table, candles were lit. My mom had pictures of her childhood lined up along the island table. I began immediately blowing the candles out and urging her to go back to sleep. I started to cry; I was terrified. I didn't know what happened to my mom or why she had these horrifying episodes. Her words pierced me. *"Oh, quit crying, Kennedy! Don't give me the guilt trip."*

I was stunned. Finally, my dad called. He somehow managed to get her to go back upstairs to sleep and told me he'd be home soon. From that day on, I carried a deep grudge. Sure, some months and seasons were better than others, but the grudge and anger I felt towards her kept coming back, especially when she acted out in front of friends and family. And yes, we called them her "moments", it was the product of extreme exhaustion, stress, and undernourishment. Well, these moments scarred me, hurt me, and confused me. I remember one of my friends seeing her when she was very sick and asking, "Does your mom have cancer?" Her body had withered so small that she looked skeletal and her eyes were so weary. If you got close enough to her, you could even smell a little alcohol. But in the final months of her life, there weren't really any episodes or moments, just my mom so weak and shriveled that eventually her liver completely failed, and she passed.

Do you want to know the first truth about love? It is patient. My dad is my superhero. My dad is love. I have never seen someone exemplify this trait of patience or tenderness so passionate like my father. He and my mom were together for seventeen years. It didn't matter what my mother said, did, experienced, or lied about, he loved her through it. When they made their vows and said, "for better or for worse," he truly meant it. There are many men who would have walked away, who would have left my mom and us. He didn't. He stayed. He loved her. He showed patience with every up and down. He helped her.

Do you know that's how Jesus loves us? No matter how far we run away from Him, no matter how much we push, or how crazy things might get, He will be there the moment we turn back because of his patience and grace.

Love is intriguing to me. When I think about marriage and relationships, the subject is honestly quite bizarre. I think it's because everyone seems to have a different perception of love. Some people spend their lives searching to find Mr. Right only to end up misunderstood and with the wrong person. We date and date more. We compare, lose feelings, fall in love, and even lose our self-control over people. Love intrigues me because every relationship is so different. There are so many different forms of love: friends, family, mates, peers, strangers, etc.

As a nineteen-year-old girl you could say I have had my fair share of relationship experiences; whether that be personal or witnessing what my friends have dealt with. One evening, I sat down with one of the women who had wrote me a letter for my 16th and 18th birthday (Sarah Webb), and soon we were in a very deep talk about boyfriends and dating. I began to cry (if you haven't learned by this point, I am a bit of a crier) because I felt like the pain that I experienced from my mother was only a nuisance in relationships. I felt like I needed to be this perfect person for my significant other, and I just wasn't meeting the expectations. I felt like I was stuck in a comparison trap with other girls. I was insecure, embarrassed of my past, and didn't know if I could ever be loved for my true self.

Sarah immediately began to cry. She told me she was so sad that I couldn't see how beautiful I was. But not physical beauty, the beauty of my heart, emotions, and spirit. She explained that it was in the broken pieces of my heart that Jesus was shining through. I didn't need to be with someone who understood my pain; I needed to be with someone who cared about my pain. She said when I chose to be with someone, it should be someone who wants to know every part of me, not just the easy and surface parts. My significant other should want to know the really, really hard things, the stuff that completely broke me, and he, too, should find it beautiful. She explained to me every relationship involves a lot of forgiveness, it's not always 50/50, neither of us are perfect.

This is how my father loved my mother. Completely, and wholeheartedly for who she was. And this is truly how Jesus Christ loves us.

We should search for this characteristic of compassion in our future mate, but ourselves too should cultivate this deeper meaning of compassion.

I think about the pain I feel when I see someone, I love hurting and sad. Then, I go onto think about how Jesus feels when he sees us suffering and in affliction. I often ponder my dad's thoughts of how it felt to lose his wife; first mentally and then physically. The longing he must have felt to help someone he loves but knowing that my mother was the person in charge of receiving help. It's a lot like how Jesus is waiting for us to turn to Him and say, "OK, I need You."

And the moment we do, things change.

It seemed like we all kept waiting for my mom to turn to all of us and say, "OK, I need your help." Instead, when my mom got sick, she pushed people away. The complete loneliness she felt as a result only made her sickness worsen. As her liver failed, so did the function of her brain. Her liver was no longer able to remove the bad toxins from her blood.

If there is one thing, I have learned from the entirety of this whole situation it is that drugs, alcohol, and mental disorders are life-altering, but love always prevails. I have learned that people will cling to excessive drinking for numerous reasons, such as shame, trauma, stress, or lack of connection. But we still can make the choice to love, forgive, and pray for them.

What has been the most eye-opening for me is seeing the general perception of alcoholics or drug addicts. These "people" are people. Just as human as you are. We put labels on others and criticize them for their "life choices" without ever taking a step back to understand why. If we were to just take a second and realize, Hey, this person is loved by Jesus just as much as I am, maybe we would put our pride aside, be humbled, and choose to love instead of judge.

This was my mom's attitude. My mom embodied the gospel of Jesus Christ like no other person I have ever met. It did not matter who someone was, she would treat the person with dignity and respect. She worked with released convicts to bring them down a path of redemption, and she worked with single parents, with people struggling with their marriage, with pastors, with teenagers, and with people of all different religions and ethnicities and cultures. Each person she met was **loved** and served. She showed me that when we choose to acknowledge a person's value with the way we treat that person, when we truly care for one another, when we love, we choose to be in the presence of God. My mom taught me that being a follower of God isn't necessarily about receiving constant attention from people around you and it isn't about being the most liked or popular. It is, however, the willingness to give and accept love.

When we don't properly receive love and community in addition to loving ourselves, our sense of identity can become totally distorted. Think about it, we crave belonging. We crave being loved and even loving others. And this craving isn't shameful. Love is what truly makes our world, our world. And it is truly what makes Jesus our Savior.

Love and community are one of the most powerful forces on earth. Think about it, people choose to join a destructive cult, organization or gang rather than being alone because we literally require community. Then we look at those who are so far away from society and never truly receive love and those tend to be the ones who lash out in violence or anger. When we move away from love and community, that's when our hearts become cold.

Think about the multitude of ways we all try to be a part of something, from clubs to teams and political parties, language, social media trends and style. We all have a drive to belong. You may have heard the saying, "Find your tribe and love them hard." We are tribal, and that's why we crave to be in one. Sometimes loving people across the country seems easier than loving the ones closest to us. But love and kindness start in our homes. Hate is taught. Be an example of love. Every kind of it. From your spouse, children, strangers, and yourself, choose love.

Proof of the power of love is that it does not die. When someone we love dies, our love for them stays. This love God has created in us reflects the love He has for us. Multiply our love on earth by a billion or so—and His love is probably even more than that. God loves us, A LOT.

Our hearts yearn for love because our Creator is love. We simply will never be satisfied in this life if we do not realize that the love we need comes from God and not the simple pleasures of earth. It is tough to understand that God's love is unconditional. He knows the worst about us yet loves us the most. God is desperately waiting for you to fall back into His arms and feel His love again. It is simply crazy to believe in anything else. You don't need to be perfect to feel this love. You just need to be you. Exactly who God created you to be. You are an object of God's love, created by His love. Some may go through their whole lives searching for love, without ever realizing that it's right in front of them, God loves us so intensely. Every heart yearns to know the love of Jesus, even if some don't realize it, everyone does.

When I think about love in my current life, as a college-age girl, the idea of love becomes a little messy. I have seen friends in life-sucking relationships, people who claimed to have found their husband or wife only to be destroyed by the relationships. I have seen the validation of love through sex and self-worth based upon "hooking up." It's funny writing these things, because I am sure some of my friends might laugh. But I think sex has become a replacement for love, and it's sad to me. I see so many people who care about the number of people they have had sex with instead of how much they truly cherished a person. I think everyone deserves someone you don't have to question, everyone deserves someone who values them and cares about their heart's souls, and dreams. We deserve someone who thinks of us more than just another body.

I've learned that sometimes people fear being vulnerable with another person because they have been hurt in the past, but these people are the ones who need authentic love the most. We turn love into a superficial game because we wonder whether any man or woman could actually love us if he or she knew who we truly were. I think therefore we turn God away, too. We are scared because we don't think anyone, or anything could possibly love us if they knew the depths of our hearts. But the truth is we are loved so deeply by a wonderful, forgiving, and graceful creator who wants you to feel love. I challenge you to believe in real love, Jesus-driven love, and respectful love, and believe that you are worthy of it.

To continue with the theme of God's love, I believe the reason I have been able to continue forward in life, down the right path without my mom here, all comes back to love: how she loved me, how my dad and family love me, how the women whose letters appear in this book have loved me, how God loves us all.

There are no silly conditions to put on love. No ifs or buts about it. Accept it and use it. Love is supposed to be expanded and given. Love is what drives us. Love makes us stronger. Love holds us together. Love changes people. Love is powerful. Loving Jesus and believing He loves us will make us love other people more. And anyone can use this gift. The truth about love; we all need it because we are created from it, by it, and for it.

Love is patient, love is kind. It does not envy, it does not boast, it is not proud. It does not dishonor others, it is not self-seeking, it is not easily angered, it keeps no record of wrongs. Love does not delight in evil but rejoices with the truth. It always protects, always trusts, always hopes, always perseveres. Love never fails.

—1 Corinthians 13:4-8, NIV

Chapter Twenty-Four

Identity and The Anorexic

It started when I was in fifth grade, the comparison with others and subsequent lack of confidence. I remember looking at certain pictures of myself with feelings of disgust and resentment. I was so grossed out by my stomach, flat chest, and awkward stance. To be completely honest, I still am sometimes. I look in the mirror and think my cheeks are too chubby, my smile is ugly or no matter how much I work out, my body is still gross. Or sometimes I just get jealous of Rachel McAdams perfect skin and smile.

I vividly remember one day when I was about eleven sitting with my mom after I told her I looked fat in my new swimsuit. Tears welled up in her eyes as we talked about body image. She told me how God had made me so brilliantly and unique. She said my body was beautiful and growing and changing every day. Tears fell from her eyes, and she hugged me tight, "Honey, you are beautiful." She taught me that beauty isn't looks. Beauty is in my heart, soul, and actions.

Body image is a weird topic. It's discussed a lot in our lives today because of social media. My thoughts on my body changed as I got older. My body was built athletically, and thicker. I ate cheeseburgers, macaroni, ice cream, and pretty much anything I wanted. I was obviously a healthy kid too, I played numerous sports, and my parents made sure I was getting the correct nutrition. However, I indulged. Social media sucked the life right out of me as I felt like I needed to validate who I was with my appearance to all my followers.

This whole "social media stage" really hit me around seventh grade, and my mom just so happened to be in the hospital again during that same time. She was so, so skinny. Social media portrayed to me that being skinny and in good shape was the definition of beauty. It seemed like everyone around me cared so much about their bodies and the way they looked. So, it was hard to believe my mom when she told me how beautiful I was, and that beauty was more than what meets the eye, because she herself seemed to be struggling with her own body image. I began to compare my body to hers, and it was the beginning of a climb over the mountain of comparison. I listened more closely to girls at school talk about having their bodies grow and change. Girls began liking boys, people had crushes, and started dating. But let's just be real, middle school is such an awkward and uncomfortable stage, and then you add to that mix social media-oh boy. Instagram, Twitter, Facebook, Snapchat were all booming. Social media only seemed to magnify my flaws. I feared days at the pool nervous that we would take pictures. I even struggled just looking in the mirror. I remained obsessed with my appearance and cared about this social media presence for years.

It seems we grow up in a system where we are taught that women (and men) are judged on their social appearance and their social graces and their value comes from what other people think and say about them. And we often find this validation through social media, video games, texting, and never in the real relationship we have with ourselves and other people. My identity was totally skewed. The validation I was using left me completely drained and insecure.

After my mom passed, I realized the reasoning for my mom's insanely skinny body wasn't really about any desire to be skinny. It seems nearly impossible to pinpoint the exact reason she struggled with this disorder; other than she couldn't control the instability around her so in turn, she controlled what and how much she was eating. Among the influences that researchers have identified as making individuals susceptible to eating disorders are genetic, biochemical, psychological, cultural, and environmental factors. Many eating disorder sufferers use food and unhealthy behaviors like dieting, starving, and bingeing and purging to cope with unpleasant and overwhelming emotions and stressful situations. It seemed like my mom at times would realize the way she was treating her body, but then coped with it by turning to alcohol.

What haunts me the most is that her alcoholism and anorexia seemed to have been avoidable issues. Yet, she isn't the only person in this world to die from something that could have been avoided. It seems like most of the time when we lose someone, we play the "what if" game. *What if I would have just said something?* Letting our minds wander until we can't bear it anymore. After going through this trauma with my mother, I have learned that our mental health and taking care of our psychological and emotional needs should be of top priority. Our sense of self is key when it comes to battling poor mental tendencies and coping issues.

For me, I feel like I'm constantly fighting a battle, and that battle is in my mind. There is a fine line between one's sense of identity, self-esteem, and mental illness. If you are at all human, you will at times struggle with these aspects of a perception of yourself, especially in a society that worships social media. It is a battle for our true identity. I am a firm believer that Jesus did not die on the cross so we could sit around, pick apart our bodies, and compare ourselves to people on Instagram.

Who do you honestly believe yourself to be? Genetics quite obviously plays a huge role in who you are. Ultimately our genes bring out the way we handle things in our environment. But ultimately, your view of yourself and the way we handle the pressures of this world begins and ends in our minds. We are always choosing the thoughts we think and the words we say about ourselves and others. Stop relying on the world to tell you who are and what your purpose should be. When we are trying to find purpose in life, why don't we first ask the One who created us? Who we believe ourselves to be essentially determines what we do with our lives. Our sense of self directs our choices. Our identity and destiny in life go hand in hand. So, when I say you aren't supposed to be created like anyone else, I mean it! You are you for a special and unique reason.

Too many times, we get stuck in a constant comparison between someone with a skinnier waistline, nicer house, prettier hair, more obedient children. God knew exactly what He was doing when He created you and the people whose paths you cross. He knew that your body would be given certain and specific abilities to move differently than anyone else does. He took the precious time to create every intricate detail on you, from the freckles on your nose to the hairs on your head. He created the exact purpose meant for your life. You look the way you look and have the abilities you have because God wanted to use our uniqueness for His glory.

Seven times in the Gospel of John, Jesus says "I am":

I am the bread of life.

I am the light of the world.

I am the door.

I am the good shepherd.

I am the resurrection and the life.

I am the way, the truth, and the life.

I am the true vine.

If we were meant to follow what Jesus did, then why do we not understand ourselves the way Jesus understood himself? And why aren't we listening to who Jesus says we are?

When I wake up in the morning, I look at myself in the mirror. I see my brown eyes, and I notice my acne, my dark circles, my bed head, and even my stinky morning breath. Most of the time, I am thinking, wow, God, you did a number on me. As I take a deep breath in and out, I remind myself that,

> I am resilient.
>
> I am growing.
>
> I am healing.
>
> I am saved.
>
> I am loved.
>
> I am a reflection of God's light.
>
> I am beautiful.

What will your "I am" be? I challenge you to look at yourself in a new way. You aren't defined by your eating disorder, your addiction, your anxiety, your physical disability, or what your boyfriend, your mother, or anyone at school says. You are you. You reflect the most beautiful and loving God. You have something special and different about you. This special thing about you will allow you to offer something different and great to our world and the people around you. You, like me, were lovingly, fearfully, and wonderfully made by God. I believe you to be a representative of light, compassion and made to be another storyteller of hope and grace.

Take a deep breath for me. Do you feel that air in your lungs? That means you were given another day...another day to be you. You need to fight for yourself and the goodness of this world. I encourage you to make a difference in this world by offering your gifts and talents to God so He can impact the world through you. The fact that you have the power in your hands to inspire, encourage, and love other people because God gave you this incredible life and story. One day, you will look deep into the eyes of our Lord, and you want to be able to have helped build His awesome kingdom and bring people to our Lord.

This goodness all starts with knowing who we are in His eyes. God knows every terrible thing we have experienced in our lives, the negative words slung at us and at others—all the things that make it so difficult for us to trust. And yet repeatedly, He extends His grace to us so we can start over and experience the beauty and the value of trusting Him. Trust that He gave each of us the body and life we have to do magnificent things in this world.

Remember that your worth is not determined by your relationship, your job, your bank account, your looks, your social media or your body. Your worth is in Jesus Christ. Your identity is not in your sin but in our Savior.

The weight you have placed on your shoulders, take it off. You don't need to be the perfect mom, wife, girlfriend, boss, or employee. You don't need to have it all together. You don't need to please everyone. You don't owe anyone anything. But you do owe yourself peace and love. You owe it to yourself to find who you are again, to be still, and to take time to breathe. You owe it to yourself to keep the promises you keep making to yourself. You owe yourself time to be alone. You owe it to yourself to stick with your goals for once; make time for those things that matter, show gratitude, workout, run a marathon, finish your book, start your business- Whatever it is you desire for your life, you owe it to yourself to pursue it. Pursue what set's your soul on fire, and never let anyone take that away from you. There is more to life than other people's opinions, Facebook, Instagram, likes, comments, popularity and materialistic commodities. There's a thing called life that needs to be lived.

I'll say it again for those who didn't catch it the first time, Jesus did not die on a cross just for us to sit around, scroll through our phones, and pick apart our flaws or compare our social media posts. We have work to do in life, lives to touch, people to love, minds to grow, families to care for, and a kingdom to serve. And I promise you, you are qualified to do these things in this exact moment. You can be a leader for our Lord right now with the faith you have, large or small.

The Christian life is not one giant high; instead it's cries out for help and forgiveness. It is experiencing mistakes and grace. It is moments of weakness, but also moments of unexplainable joy.

If you don't see the greatness of God, then yes, all the things money can buy can seem very exciting. Just like if you never saw the sun, a lamp might seem overwhelmingly bright. Turning our backs on God can cause us to fall in love with things that are only temporary pleasures. If we never realize the truth God speaks about us and never understand the time and love He put into us, then we might fall to the words, perspectives, and judgments of those who don't matter.

I hope you come to know that happiness was never about your job, your money, your outfits, your degree, or being in a relationship. Happiness was never about following the latest trends on Instagram and Facebook. It was never about how many Likes or Comments you get. These are all temporary placeholders in our lives. Joy is found in the discovery of your true self; it's found in listening to your heart and the words the Holy Spirit whispered into it. Happiness is about being a little kinder to yourself, embracing the person you are slowly becoming, learning to love and live with yourself. That happiness is not in the hands of other people; but your very own. It's always been about you and the kingdom of God inside you.

When we fuel our minds with the healthy choices, our lives in turn become healthy. One of the greatest powers we all hold is the ability to control our thoughts and, even better, have God guide our thoughts.

When we feed our minds with positive, Jesus-guided, genuine thoughts, our outlook and perceptions change. We become more comfortable with where we are and who we are. I encourage you to look beyond the trivial things of life, and dive into what makes you, *you*. Learn to be your own friend first.

We are all struggling to figure ourselves out. We are nervous and anxious about exposing our souls and identities to the people around us and even to God. But, at the exact same time we desperately need help to guide us on this self-exploration journey. Jesus once said that the kingdom of God is within us;

20 One day the Pharisees asked Jesus, "When will the Kingdom of God begin?" Jesus replied, "The Kingdom of God isn't ushered in with visible signs. 21 You won't be able to say, 'It has begun here in this place or there in that part of the country.' For the Kingdom of God is within you." Luke 17:20-21 TLB

Yet most of us don't even bother to explore the possibility that this might be true. We have an opportunity to find God within us. I hope you choose this path. Engage in the exploration of your identity, and through your walk with Jesus, I hope you find out just who you truly are.

Your identity directly correlates with your purpose. Because what you believe yourself to be also determines what you do with your life. Whatever it might be, God has placed a passion within you. I always thought that if it's my passion, then I must be the absolute best at it. This thinking is all wrong. You don't have to be the best at whatever it is you're passionate about; you just must be willing to surrender this passion and gift to God.

You can choose to live in His freedom. Not because you are a perfect person, with an easy passion and talent, but because God is sovereign, and He says in the Bible that we can live free from self-doubt and fear when we put our trust and purpose in who He says we are. This perspective can change everything we do, and the outcome of our lives.

I thank the women who wrote these letters to me, they were so candid and honest with me, and that was like a breath of fresh air. They showed me that it takes courage and bravery to be my most authentic self, but when I am, that's when I feel the most beautiful inside and out. I am no longer obsessed with comparison, but instead captivated by my purpose because I know who I am in God.

Chapter Twenty-Five

The Security of Pain

In the weeks after my mom died, I would get this awful anxiety. My older brother had just left for college, and I remember waking up in the middle of the night thinking he was dead. I woke to similar middle-of-the-night anxiety attacks about pretty much every person I loved. The pain I felt from losing my mom has caused me to become terrified that at any moment the people I love would die. I was afraid of losing someone close to me again. But the thing about this anxiety was that it was true. We really can lose the people we love any day, at any time. The more we love people, the harder it is to think about losing them. I became extremely insecure about my surroundings and myself because I wasn't finding my security in God. I wasn't letting God heal my pain. I wasn't listening to the words he was speaking into my heart. I was so focused on my anxieties and people dying, I forgot about the strength and timing God has. I forgot about what scripture says about my pain and uncertainty.

Romans 5:3-4 ESV:

"... but we rejoice in our sufferings, knowing that suffering produces endurance, and endurance produces character, and character produces hope,"

In the times I suffered and chose to rely on God, I grew stronger. I learned how to handle my anxiety and fears the right way. I now realize that God seems to be doing ten thousand things and I am only aware of two, if any. When I feel pain, I now know that God is working on something much bigger. I have shifted my worrying about "bad things" happening in my life because I am not in control of what happens, but God is. And I trust Him fully to use my situations to ultimately bring glory back to Him and make me stronger. That's where I find security in my pain. It's in my suffering, that I have someone there for me who refuses to let go of me, who loves me deeper than any of my wounds, who takes care of me, and protects me at all costs.

It was tough when I felt sad about my mom because it seemed like everyone else in life just had it going for them (or at least their social media said so). I was a very anxious, insecure, scared girl. When I find myself in this negative anxious cycle, it's usually because I am spending too much time with social media, gossip, and partying. Sometimes we need to reevaluate where we are, to take a step back and refocus on Jesus. There is nothing wrong with stepping away for a moment to find who you are again.

I have noticed how important it is for me to understand my pain. When something hurts me, I always reflect on why that specific thing bothers me, and why it is causing me heartache. Understanding my pain has helped me know what I can do to cope with negativity and allowed me to nourish my positive qualities. Meditation has been a crucial part of getting through my mental obstacles, just letting thoughts come and go. It's significant to understand what causes certain emotions whether those be happy or sad emotions, they play an important role in our lives. Understanding these feelings can help us funnel out the things that don't actually matter and focus on uncovering the underlying issues. For me it was counseling, talking to mentors, being honest about how I was feeling, praying, journaling, and spending an immense amount of time getting to know myself and who I was in Him all allowed me to hit the Reset button, realign, and find myself again.

I believe in the power of realignment. Sometimes things will fall apart to make way for a new you to emerge. You don't always understand why, in fact you don't really need to. Just being confident that things are aligning for a greater good. Have faith that things will get better, because they always do.

During this transformative process following my mother's death, I also learned about the stigma around mental health issues. I went through it firsthand with my mother. She was ashamed and scared of what other people would think of her if they knew she was suffering mentally. She had an addiction, but see, most of us do. Whether it be, Instagram, binge-watching Netflix, working out, eating, shopping, etc. These things detach us from our reality and give us the feeling just for those mere moments, that everything is okay. We use these things to numb our pain because they're comfortable and easy. It's easy to wake up and put the mask on and say we're fine, say we're strong, say we don't need help, but do we mean it? It's a terrifying thought to live outside of your comfort zone, it's a terrifying thought to ask for guidance, for help, and it's even terrifying to look ourselves in the mirror and admit to our issues. But, outside that comfort zone in those terrifying times is where we can lean on God, and it's where we grow, learn, and climb mountains. It's where we become ourselves, inspirations, and encouragers. As I have said a million times before in my book, it all starts with what we fuel our minds with every single day. What you believe about yourself and your life is what you live out daily. Become mindful of your values, beliefs, and morals, these things hold great power over our lives. I urge to come to understand your emotions. Learn to feel and cope with them. It's scary because sometimes doing that can cause changes in your life, and that's when you start focusing on what you might lose instead of what you could gain. But trust that your pain is just a part of the process of becoming who you are called to be.

There was time when I decided I needed to make a change in my life. So, I determined that I was going to be so busy loving myself and God that I wouldn't be distracted by my self-doubt and anxiety. At first, it worked. But then it seemed like the more I wanted for my life, the more I chased, and the less satisfied I became. My idea of my life wasn't fully aligned with what God was calling me to do. I was working hard at these surface-level dreams and dissatisfied with where I was. God was pushing me to go deeper and telling me to enjoy each moment as it happens. I learned to find in the here and now and enjoy the process of becoming who He called me to be and who I wanted to be. Even in the moments it seemed really hard, I began to ask God, "what do you want me to learn here?" "what do you want me to see?". These questions were the last things I wanted to ask, because sometimes the answers were painful to know. But, anything great in life comes with hard work and sometimes a little pain. I knew that every morning when I woke up, I still had purpose. I was alive and breathing. I was given another day to fight the good fight. It occurred to me that all the things God was asking me to do required discipline and to be stretched in directions I have never been.

A stronger body? Working out (even when I didn't want to) and repeating that painful "No" to my favorite dessert.

A better spiritual life? Disciplining myself to wake up early for prayer and meditation, finding time to journal or to be still in the presence of Jesus.

More money? Working extra hours, doing things no one else would in order to achieve my financial goals so I can pay for college without a loan.

Less insecurity and anxiety? Reaching out for help, even though it might have felt embarrassing and scary.

Pain is required for growth. Pain shapes us. When we use our pain in the right way, it helps us grow, changes us, and allows us to connect with others. And isn't that what life is all about—human connection? Has it ever occurred to you maybe that's why we belong in community? We are supposed to help each other. We understand everyone in our life's experiences pain in some way, to some degree. We can't choose the stress that comes our way at the worst possible time, but we can choose how we move forward. We can choose kindness, compassion, love, and generosity. After all, why would we not choose to love and comfort those around us when we know how meaningful those gestures can be?

When life gets tiresome and hard, don't jump to the conclusion that God is hanging you out to dry and abandoning you. Don't fall to the idea that there is no God. Instead, rejoice that you are in the midst of pain with your Savior.

Here is what Peter said about difficult times:

"Beloved friends, if life gets extremely difficult, with many tests, don't be bewildered as though something strange were overwhelming you. Instead, continue to rejoice, for you, in a measure, have shared in the sufferings of the Anointed One so that you can share in the revelation of his glory and celebrate with even greater gladness!" 1 Peter 4:12-13, TPT

I know that growth in the right direction is a process, it might hurt, but I also know through any of that pain, I have a redeemer.

When I was young, I remember learning in Sunday School about a butterfly analogy. I can't remember the exact message, but for some reason the butterfly stuck with me. When I entered college, the butterfly imagery came back. I noticed it in books or articles I read, in songs, and walking through campus or in nature. My close friend lost her grandmother, and numerous times a butterfly would show up and it reminded them that their grandmother was always with them. The butterfly symbolism was everywhere. So, I got to thinking about a butterfly and the metamorphosis process, and the overall intrigue and beauty of a butterfly. The butterfly taught me an extraordinary message. It taught me that, change ensures growth. When the caterpillar changes to the butterfly, it can never go back. Just like how when we put our lives, trust, and hope in Jesus, God will make us new creations and our hearts will be forever changed. When you come to Him, you allow Him to completely recreate you. We all begin at a starting point. We then begin to fuel ourselves, just like a caterpillar eating and eating until it's ready to go in its cocoon. When the caterpillar breaks out of its cocoon, it's a miracle, it changes entire structure to a completely different being. This is what God can make of us when we choose to break out of our cocoons with His help. The process is not always easy, but I encourage you to engage in the beautiful struggle of breaking out of the cocoon and become the butterfly. Let go of everything that's weighing you down, let the pain make your wings stronger, and fly. Breaking out is painful, frustrating, and laborious. You might even wonder, 'is this really worth it?' but it is. It always is. Growth is uncomfortable because you've never been that version of yourself, give yourself the abundant grace God has for you and enjoy the beauty of becoming.

I remember the first time someone mentioned to me about how I should write a book. I laughed out loud. I was only 17. But, a part of me just wondered "what if I actually did?", so I sat down to write, expecting God to take control of my hands and just type everything He needed me to write. When in reality, it has been one of the most painful and frustrating processes for me. I had to take huge steps out of my comfort zone and let my mind, heart, and soul be stretched to another level and it pushed me to grow forward into God's hands. It eventually became a therapy for me to write. So, I started my blog 'Dear Kennedy'. The feedback I got from my first few posts fueled me to continue to write my book. This whole little story is about the overwhelming idea of keep going, keep trusting.

There are 10 things I try to practice as much as I can, even though it's sometimes hard, but these things have helped me overcome so many obstacles in my short life, so far.

1. Stop complaining and focus on my blessings.

2. Embrace loneliness.

3. Turn off my phone.

4. Sweat every day.

5. Fail forward.

6. Acknowledge mistakes and ask for forgiveness.

7. Let go of things I can't control.

8. Set boundaries

9. Avoid gossip and bashing others.

10. Keep my faith larger than my fears.

You are being presented with a choice, to evolve or remain. Everything in your life is the result of a choice you make; if you want a different outcome, make a different choice. Choosing to remain means you will continue to battle the same problems, the same routine, the same results. Until you choose to evolve, you will stagnate. Until you choose to love yourself a little harder and say no to the things that keep you down, you will remain unchanged. Until you choose to use your failures to depend on God more deeply, you will remain the same. Trust yourself enough to know God is in your heart and moving you.

Closeness to God and finding His grace is not an emotion, a memory, or a set of circumstances. It is a daily devotion and practice to listen to what He is calling you to do. It is tough. But it's better than remaining in your old and draining ways, because those old ways will not be opening any new doors. In between those goals, there is a little thing that should be enjoyed, it's called life. Choosing a new path sometimes will be tough and tiring and will make you weary, but it's worth it.

I had to keep trusting. I had to keep hoping. If I didn't have my faith, which my parents instilled in me years ago, there was no possible way I could even rationalize the heartbreak of losing my mom. I wouldn't be able to even begin to comprehend the importance of mental health and the effects of mental illness.

To think that we can love God without ever being changed by Him is to think you can jump into the ocean and not get wet. When we really love Him, we must understand that sometimes He might wreck life as we know it, but He never fails to build it up again into something beautiful, lasting, and extraordinary. If we have insecurities and experience pain, that also means we have the opportunity to immerse ourselves deeply into God's word, will, plan, and strength. Don't give up on your dream, or your next steps. Become the butterfly and take flight.

Chapter Twenty-Six

Brotherly Love

Death can be an awkward topic. I was in middle school when my mom died so you can imagine some of the uncomfortable situations I encountered. From weird Facebook messages to classmates randomly asking questions about it, or some people imposing their opinions about the afterlife. One great lesson I have learned through the death of my mom was to never equate my experience with anyone else's. We all experience pain, death, and hurt in a different way. Even the people closest to me, my brothers and father, handled my mom passing differently.

The thought of growing up and not having my mom by my side taunted me. It scared me that I had to adjust and take on a new role in life. I had to be strong even when I felt like the world around me was already gone. I don't really know why I felt like this because I have the most incredible support system at home. I am completely surrounded by family that would be there for me without question: Aunt Julie, Uncle Mike, Uncle Gordy, my Grandpa, Aunt Marissa, Aunt Cathy, Aunt Nancy, Aunt Kris, Cousin Kim, Uncle Pat ...well, you get the point; I am blessed.

After we lost my mom my older brother, Parker, and younger brother, Karson, became and remain my best friends. Our lives together changed quickly: laundry, dishes, cleaning, finding rides to and from practices, study habits, relationships, and honestly, for me sometimes just getting along with the three boys in the house. Her death continued to draw us closer together after we each continuously faced adjustments and changes. It felt like we had gone to war together, and there was no way I was going to lose either of them. It didn't matter how bad the fights got between us three, or what words we said to each other, we were there for each other in a heartbeat.

My brothers have played a vital part in the woman I am and the woman I am becoming. It is all about the perspective that they have taught me. Guys are wired differently than girls—in particular, the things they care about versus what I think I should care about. They are never scared to tell me how it is, straight up, and honestly. Anytime I cried over a boy or stupid girl drama in front of them, they always found a way to make me laugh or smile. Siblings are special. I want to share with you the advice they have taught me that has helped me to grow and become who I am.

If you want to live a life full of joy and excitement, live like my older brother Parker. He never shies away from adventure. Parker spent one summer living and working at Yellowstone National park, studied abroad in Ireland, went four-wheeling through the deserts of Morocco, and visited friends in Spain. He's also been on two mission trips to the Bahamas and explored Ecuador, Algeria, Serbia, Mexico, Canada, and Columbia. Not to mention, he's traveled throughout most of the U.S. Everywhere he goes, he tackles a new adventure head-on. My younger brother and I joke about how perfect he is and that we have never met someone who doesn't like him. He literally radiates happiness. He makes the best out of every circumstance and always chooses to fall in love with every moment his life has to offer.

Parker has taught me that if it excites you and scares you (and is legal), then you should probably do it. He lives by the "scare" philosophy, and he encourages me to do something that scares me every single week. His mantra has rubbed off and allowed me to fall in love with the journey of life. Life truly is an exploration to find ourselves. Parker teaches me courage. He shows me that courage doesn't mean we aren't afraid; it means we don't let fear stop us. But my favorite thing about Parker is that he loves people. He is a lot like my mom in that way. The cultures he has experienced, friends he's made, and people he has encountered have all been touched by him. He can connect with people instantly and always loves to learn from their lives and words. He never stops learning because he knows his life will never stop teaching.

My younger brother Karson is so, so special. I know it might sound like I am bragging, but wow. Karson was gifted with artistic and music capabilities I would kill for. He had a tough time with some bullies and identity issues before and after my mom passed. There is nothing in this world that makes me angrier than entitled kids tearing down other peers for having a different skill set. But Karson has never, ever let anyone discourage his dreams or goals. Karson teaches me the strength of maturity and how to be the bigger person. There had been times he faced a bully, but he always chose to take the higher road. One time specifically, when he was only fifteen, responded to the insensitive comments by saying, "Obviously, if you feel the need to say those things, you're going through a tough time in life. I just want you to know I have already forgiven you and I will be praying for you." I on the other hand had trouble controlling my temper when it came to people hurting my little brother. It felt like it was my job to protect him from any pain. My older brother was the same way, us three had each other's backs no matter what. Karson taught me the power of maturity. He knew at such a young age that not every situation needs a reaction. If we do react, we're not likely to change anything. We probably won't make people apologize or act kinder by shouting or getting angry. Sometimes it's better to just let things be, to choose not to chase answers and not fight for "getting even" with a person because all that is in God's hands.

Karson is confident and determined to make something of his life. He never cares what other people are saying. He has so much faith in our Lord, that other opinions do not faze him. There have been other times where people have mad insensitive comments about his decision to focus on his art and music, but Karson always stood firmly in his choices and in his faith.

Karson can leave us all with the theme of passion. It isn't just some fluke that God has placed a certain passion in your heart; the passion is your calling. Karson chases his dreams fearlessly, inspiring me to find what sets my soul on fire. He creates an escape from reality with his music and art and pushes himself to grow deeper and find meaning in his work.

Overall, I have been beyond blessed to have Parker and Karson as my brothers. I can't imagine going through life without them. I hope you learn from their lifestyles the way I did. I hope you take a step outside your comfort zone and follow what sets your soul on fire, just like these two do.

Chapter Twenty-Seven

Holding On

I clutched my mother's hand tightly as a tear rolled down my cheek. I could hardly bear to look at her weak body on the hospital bed. My jaw tensed as I tried to hold back from crying. The room seemed to be spinning. I noticed the breathing tube lined across her face and the medical devices keeping her alive.

How did it come to this?

I tried my best to tell her to keep fighting, that I loved her and needed her. I held on to the thought of her getting healthy again and coming back home and inspiring our whole community. I held on to the idea that God wouldn't put us through anything more than we had already faced.

Two weeks later, she passed.

Fast forward to this day, and that moment in the hospital still haunts me, and probably always will. It almost feels like a bad dream. I think about who I was when my mom was here on earth and realize I was just so young and still her baby. What hurts worse is thinking about the future. She won't be here on my wedding day, graduations, heartbreaks, celebrations. She won't be here for the little moments when I just need to vent and cry, for the boy talk, girl drama, encouraging texts, or funny jokes. She isn't here anymore.

But, I am. And I am holding on. I am holding on to the faith, strength, and courage she instilled in me. I am holding on to the letters and advice these women wrote to me. I am holding on to my father, friends, and family. I am letting go of what I can't change, moving forward, but never forgetting. I am allowing the pain to build me and grow me. I am blessed to be alive and fighting the good fight.

I have the opportunity to create a better life, to make an impact on those around me, and live out my mother's legacy. I hope to encourage you to do the same.

When I feel envious of those who seem to have it all, I remember that they struggle too. Our struggles and battles might be different, but everyone has them. Every family has dysfunction, everybody feels pain, everybody hurts others sometime in their lives. We all mess up, and we all fall short of the glory of God. But we do all have power—the power of kindness and love. It's a decision we can make every day to love the way Jesus loves us and to offer forgiveness, a helping hand, a shoulder to cry on, and a listening ear, all without our own personal judgments. We can always appreciate those around us and say our "I love you's" and "thank you's." If I had a second chance, I would make sure that every day my mother knew how much I loved her. When we truly give to others in that way, when we choose love over animosity, it not only makes those around us feel cared for and appreciated, but it also develops our own inner peace and happiness. If you really want to be happy in life, be thankful. **Life is precious.**

***

Dear whoever is reading this,

The past you is overflowing with so much pride looking at how far you've come and the ideas you have to continue to grow yourself. Your problems may feel insurmountable while you're in the middle of them. Sometimes your emotions might even take over, and you'll lose your sense of self. But remember, there is no event bigger than your ability to respond to it. You have power in your response. You have power in your choice. You have power in you, and even more power from the kingdom of God within you.

Trust that.

***

Thank you to my readers.

Where do I even begin?

I wouldn't be here without all of you. It's been my dream to be an author, and I am so thankful that you took your time to read about my journey.

There were times I questioned "will anyone actually read this?" Then as I dove deeper into my book, and into my story, I realized I needed to because everyone has a story that deserves to be heard. My mother believed that, and it's true. We all have a story, wisdom to give, and lesson to teach.

I published this book before I turned 20. You need to understand that I am still so young and growing (and if I can pursue my dreams this young so can you). I hope that my book gave you a little insight and encouragement. I have learned in my short life, I don't know when my last day on earth is, so me making a difference in this world starts now.

I encourage my readers to live with intention. Share your story. Be kind. Love passionately. Forgive often. Be the light. Find God. Be the butterfly and take flight.

Thank you again for reading. I appreciate way more than you know.

2 Corinthians 12:9 NIV

But he said to me, "My grace is sufficient for you, for my power is made perfect in weakness." Therefore, I will boast all the more gladly about my weaknesses, so that Christ's power may rest on me.

With so much love,

Kennedy Marleen Leighton

☐

Made in the USA
Monee, IL
15 February 2020